HISTORICAL TOURS

GETTYSBURG

HELP US KEEP THIS GUIDE UP TO DATE

We would love to hear from you concerning your experiences with this guide and how you feel it could be improved and kept up to date. Please send your comments and suggestions to:

editorial@GlobePequot.com

Thanks for your input, and happy travels!

HISTORICAL TOURS

GETTYSBURG

Trace the Path of America's Heritage

RANDI MINETOR

With an introduction by James C. Bradford

Photographs by Nic Minetor

Guilford, Connecticut

An imprint of Rowman & Littlefield

Distributed by NATIONAL BOOK NETWORK

Copyright © 2015 by Rowman & Littlefield

Maps by Daniel Lloyd © Rowman & Littlefield
Historical interior map on p. 92 courtesy of the Library of Congress.

All photographs by Nic Minetor, except for the following: Photos on pp. 1, 2, 5, 9, 10-17, 31 (bottom), 34, 44, 51, 52, 56, 58, 61, 71, 73, 75, 79, 80, 91, and 95 courtesy of the Library of Congress; photo of General Robert E. Lee on p. 16 courtesy of Alexander Gardner, from the Library of Congress; photos on pp. 82 and 96 courtesy of the National Park Service; photo on p. v © Shutterstock.

British Library Cataloguing in Publication Information Available

Library of Congress Cataloging-in-Publication Data Available

ISBN 978-1-4930-1295-4 (pbk.)
ISBN 978-1-4930-1777-5 (e-book)

∞™ The paper used in this publication meets the minimum requirements of American National Standard for Information Sciences—Permanence of Paper for Printed Library Materials, ANSI/NISO Z39.48-1992.

All the information in this guidebook is subject to change. We recommend that you call ahead to obtain current information before traveling. All restaurants are open daily for breakfast, lunch, and dinner, unless otherwise noted.

Contents

Introduction

by JAMES C. BRADFORD

The Battle of Gettysburg marked the high
tide of the Confederate war effort in the
Civil War and proved to be the turning point
of the war in the east. It was fought in July
1863, two and a half years after Southern
states began seceding from the Union in
reaction to the election of Abraham Lincoln,
whose ascent to power—along with that of
his fellow Republicans—threatened South-
erners' interpretations of the U.S. Constitu-
tion and the institution of slavery. The battle
ended the last major Confederate invasion
of the North and resulted in the loss by

This famous portrait of Abraham Lincoln
was taken by Alexander Gardner on
November 8, 1863.

the Army of Northern Virginia of so many men, wagons, and horses that its
commander, General Robert E. Lee, could never again launch a strategic
offensive.

The Setting

The road to Gettysburg was littered with thousands of dead from both North
and South and the destruction of the reputations of commanding officers
in both armies. Indeed, the spring of 1863 marked the start of the third and
pivotal year of the Civil War as belligerents on both sides grew weary of the
conflict and its attendant loss of lives.

During the previous twelve months, Union armies had attempted to
advance on the Confederate capital at Richmond, Virginia, first from the
southeast and then from the north. In March 1862 Major General George B.
McClellan launched the Peninsula Campaign, which was designed to outflank
Confederate defenses in northern Virginia and to attack from the southeast.
Using 389 vessels, the Union commander moved the 146,000-man Army
of the Potomac by water from Alexandria and Annapolis to Fort Monroe, on
the tip of the peninsula formed by the York and James Rivers. When they

Published in 1887 by L. Prang & Co., this unknown artist's interpretation of the Confederate army's advance at Gettysburg provides a sense of the battle's size and scope.

arrived, however, Major General John B. Magruder's 13,000 Confederates ended Yankee hopes of a quick victory when they checked the advance of McClellan's army at a series of earthworks they had hastily erected across the peninsula. General Joseph E. Johnston soon arrived to take overall command of Confederate forces in the Battle of Seven Pines (May 31), during which Johnston was injured. Robert E. Lee took command of Confederate forces and launched a series of offenses, the Seven Days Battles (June 25 to July 1, 1862) that led McClellan to retreat and President Lincoln to order the Army of the Potomac back to Washington.

With Richmond safe from the southeast, Lee rushed forces north to fend off an attack from the north by the Army of Virginia, led by Major General John Pope. A series of brilliant tactical moves by Lee culminated in the Second Battle of Manassas (August 28–30, 1862), a defeat so complete that the Army of Virginia was disbanded, its forces transferred to the Army of the Potomac and its commander, Pope, transferred to the Army's Department of

CIVIL WAR TIMELINE	1860		1861	
	November 6 Abraham Lincoln elected president.	**December 20** South Carolina secedes from the Union. Mississippi, Alabama, Florida, Georgia, Louisiana, and Texas follow within two months.	**February 9** Confederate States of America (C.S.A.) forms, with Jefferson Davis as president.	**April 12** Fort Sumter attacked by Confederate army. **April 17** Virginia secedes, followed by Arkansas, Tennessee, and North Carolina. **April 20** Robert E. Lee resigns his commission in the U.S. Army.

the Northwest in Milwaukee, Wisconsin. Confederate commander Robert E. Lee then reversed the tables on his Union opponents and crossed the Potomac River into Maryland, where he was defeated at the Battle of Antietam (Sharpsburg) (September 17,1862) and forced to return to Virginia.

Displeased with McClellan's failure to pursue Lee, President Lincoln turned command of the Army of the Potomac over to Major General Ambrose E. Burnside, who launched the third major Union thrust of the year on Richmond. Moving southeastward to bypass Lee's defenses in northern Virginia, Burnside crossed the Rappahannock River at Fredericksburg, only to be thrown back across the river with great losses (December 11–13, 1862).

West of the Allegheny Mountains, campaigning appeared equally inconclusive, if not quite as sanguinary. The new year of 1862 opened with Union forces capturing Fort Henry on the Tennessee River (February 6) and Fort Donelson on the Cumberland (February 16), but when they moved south under the command of Major General Ulysses S. Grant, they were checked at Shiloh near Pittsburg Landing (April 6) by Confederate forces commanded by General Albert Sidney Johnston, and forced to withdraw. That same month a Union army commanded by Brigadier General John Pope occupied Island No. 10 in Tennessee (April 7, 1862), and a Union naval squadron commanded by Flag Officer David G. Farragut took control of New Orleans (April 25, 1862), but Confederate forces retained command of the Mississippi River at Port Hudson and Vicksburg.

In 1863 campaigning opened in the west with the Union maneuvering against the Confederate citadel at Vicksburg, resulting in a siege that began in May and continued into early July, finally resulting in a resounding Union victory for Major General Ulysses S. Grant. Meanwhile, in the east, the Army of the Potomac, now commanded by Major General Joseph Hooker, moved

1862

| July 21 Battle of Bull Run (First Manassas) | November 1 President Lincoln appoints George B. McClellan general-in-chief of the U.S. armed forces. | January 31 Lincoln issues General War Order No. 1, calling for U.S. forces to advance by February 22. | February 6 Major General Ulysses S. Grant captures Fort Henry in Tennessee, and Fort Donelson ten days later. | April 6 and 7 Confederates surprise Grant at Shiloh; 23,000 men are killed or wounded in the fighting.

April 24 Flag Officer David Farragut leads seventeen Union ships to take New Orleans. |

again to outflank Lee's Army of Northern Virginia just west of Fredericksburg—only to suffer a demoralizing defeat at Chancellorsville (May 2–3) that
left the Union high command in shambles. When word reached Lee that the
5,000 Federal troops at West Point (June 2) had withdrawn down the York
River to Fort Monroe, he concluded that the Confederate capital was safe
from that direction and began laying plans to invade the North by moving
west of Washington to strike a decisive blow in Pennsylvania.

The Approach to Gettysburg

Following the death of Thomas "Stonewall" Jackson at Chancellorsville, Lee
had reorganized his army into three corps, under Generals James Longstreet,
Richard S. Ewell, and A. P. Hill, and had begun planning for the offensive
he now judged possible. Leaving Hill's corps opposite the Federal army
on the Rappahannock, Lee sent those of Longstreet and Ewell toward the
Blue Ridge Mountains and into the Shenandoah Valley to turn northward
across Maryland and into Pennsylvania. Receiving reports that Lee was on
the move, Hooker ordered Major General Alfred Pleasanton, two divisions
of cavalry, and a brigade of infantry to reconnoiter the area around Culpep-
per, Virginia. Near Brandy Station (June 9) they met Major General J. E. B.
Stuart and his Confederate cavalry, whom Lee had positioned to protect the
flank of the units moving toward the Blue Ridge. In the largest predominately
cavalry engagement in North American history, the two forces fought to a
tactical draw; however, it amounted to a strategic victory for the Confederates because the Union forces withdrew without disrupting the movements
of Lee's main army. Regardless of the outcome, Stuart had been caught

1862

May 31	June 1	July 11	August 29–30	September 4–9
Battle of Seven Pines: Confederate General Joseph Johnston attacks near Richmond; the battle is inconclusive.	General Robert E. Lee replaces Johnston and assumes command of the Confederate army.	General Henry Halleck becomes general-in-chief of the Union army.	Second Manassas: Generals James Longstreet and Stonewall Jackson defeat the Union Army of the Potomac.	The Confederate army invades Harper's Ferry, West Virginia.

June 25–July 1
The Seven Days Battle near Richmond; McClellan begins withdrawal from the South.

September 17
Battle of Antietam: 26,000 men are dead or wounded by day's end.

September 18
Lee's army crosses the Potomac, withdrawing that evening to Virginia.

September 22
Lincoln issues a preliminary Emancipation Proclamation.

by surprise, and memory of that embarrassment would influence his later actions.

As Ewell's II Corps slipped into the Shenandoah Valley, crossed the Potomac at Williamsport and Shepherdstown, and entered Pennsylvania, Lincoln rejected Hooker's

The Seventeenth New York Battery served from August 1862 through June 1865 in defense of Washington, DC. Captain George T. Anthony remained in command of this unit throughout its service.

plan to strike at Hill's isolated corps at Fredericksburg and follow with another attack on the Confederate capital. Instead, the president ordered Hooker to keep his army between the main Confederate army and Washington, saying, "Lee's army, and not Richmond, is your true objective point. If he comes toward the Upper Potomac, follow on his flank, and . . . [f]ight him when opportunity offers." When Lincoln also rejected Hooker's request for approval to evacuate Harper's Ferry, Hooker tendered his resignation, prob-ably expecting its rejection. But Lincoln accepted, and on July 28 Major General George G. Meade replaced Hooker as commander of the Army of the Potomac.

Reaching Chambersburg in Pennsylvania, Ewell divided his corps, sending

1863

November 7
Lincoln replaces McClellan with Major General Ambrose Burnside.

December 13
Burnside is roundly defeated at Fredericksburg.

January 1
Lincoln issues the formal Emancipation Proclamation, freeing all slaves in Confederate territories.

January 25
Lincoln replaces Burnside with Major General Joseph Hooker.

May 1-4
Lee defeats Hooker at Chancellorsville; Stonewall Jackson is wounded and dies on May 10.

Lieutenant General Jubal Early east to sever rail and telegraph lines linking Baltimore and Harrisburg while he continued northeastward to Carlisle. Meanwhile, Longstreet's Third Corps reached Chambersburg. Thus, by June 28, Lee's army was deployed in a 60-mile-long arch from his headquarters in Chambersburg northeastward to Carlisle, then southeastward to York. Roughly equidistant roads led from all three towns directly to Gettysburg. When a spy informed Lee that Meade had moved his Army of the Potomac to Frederick, Maryland, the Confederate commander concluded it was time to concentrate his forces and ordered them to converge on Cashtown. But it was at Gettysburg, 5 miles east of Cashtown, where ten roads converged from all directions, that units of both armies would come together over the next three days to engage in the bloodiest battle of the Civil War and its turning point in the East.

Aftermath

After four days of combat, casualties were horrid on both sides:

	Union	Confederate	Total
Killed and Wounded			
July 1	5,400	5,600	11,000
July 2	9,000	6,000	15,000
July 3	3,300	4,700	8,000
Captured and Missing	5,400	5,200	10,600
TOTAL	23,100	21,500	44,600

When the casualties over the following three days of Lee's retreat and Meade's pursuit are included, the total rises to about 51,000.

1863

June 3
Lee begins his march to the North, entering Pennsylvania with 75,000 soldiers.

June 28
Lincoln replaces Hooker with Major General George Meade.

July 1–3
Meade defeats Lee at Gettysburg, turning the tide of the war.

July 4
A six-week siege at Vicksburg ends with Confederate surrender to Grant.

September 19–20
The Union Army of the Cumberland becomes trapped in Chattanooga, Tennessee, when it is defeated at Chickamauga.

October 16
Lincoln appoints Grant commander of the West.

November 19
Soldiers National Cemetery is dedicated at Gettysburg; Lincoln gives the Gettysburg Address.

November 23–25
The Union army finally defeats the Confederates under General Braxton Bragg at Chattanooga.

Neither commander considered renewing the battle on July 4, and that night Lee began withdrawing southwestward toward Fairfield, crossing South Mountain and heading home to Virginia. Learning of Lee's departure, Meade set out in cautious pursuit. Not wishing to engage Lee in the rugged terrain of South Mountain, Meade remained to the east until turning westward through Turner's and Crampton's Gaps. By the time he did pursue, it was too late to engage Lee, who had crossed the Potomac River on a pontoon bridge hastily erected at Falling Waters, south of Williamsport on the night of July 13–14. Learning Lee had eluded him, Meade halted pursuit and the Gettysburg Campaign was over. Never again would Robert E. Lee and his Army of Northern Virginia be able to mount an offensive on such a scale.

Lincoln was pleased with the Union victory at Gettysburg, but disappointed by Meade's failure to engage Lee as he withdrew and escaped back into Virginia. The failure of Lee's invasion and the surrender of Vicksburg to Union forces on July 4, the day fighting ended at Gettysburg, convinced many Europeans that the Confederacy could not win the war, but the huge loss of life led many Northerners to question the cost of subduing the South and contributed to the outbreak of riots against the draft that rocked New York City, July 11–16. Despite Lincoln's disappointment in what he considered Meade's failure to aggressively pursue Lee, Meade was promoted to brigadier general in the regular army and Congress passed a resolution commending Meade and the Army of the Potomac "for the skill and heroic valor which at Gettysburg repulsed, defeated, and drove back, broken and dispirited . . . the veteran army of the rebellion."

In the aftermath of the campaign, Confederate President Jefferson Davis rejected Lee's offer to resign as commander of the Army of Northern Virginia.

Introduction

1864

March 9
Lincoln appoints Grant general in chief.

May 5–6 and 8–12
Battles in Wilderness and Spotsylvania turn the war in the Union's favor; Major General William Sherman begins a march to Atlanta with 100,000 men.

June 15
The nine-month Union siege of Petersburg begins.

During the remainder of 1863, Lee consistently outmaneuvered Meade. At the start of the 1864 campaigning season, Lincoln named U. S. Grant, the victor at Vicksburg, commander of all U.S. armies. Grant maintained his headquarters with those of Meade and the Army of the Potomac for the remainder of the war. In Grant, Lincoln had finally found a general who would tenaciously drive the Confederates into surrender.

This Hallowed Ground

Contemporaries understood the significance of the Battle of Gettysburg and the ground on which it was fought. In the immediate aftermath of the battle, 20,000 wounded soldiers were treated at Camp Letterman General Hospital, a makeshift cluster of tents erected east of Gettysburg, then transferred to permanent hospitals in Baltimore, Washington, and Philadelphia. Thousands of graves remained scattered across the fields that encircled the town, so many that residents worked with state officials to establish a Soldiers' National Cemetery. On November 19, 1863, officials came from Washington to dedicate the new cemetery located, appropriately, on Cemetery Hill. President Abraham Lincoln miscalculated when he predicted in his Gettysburg Address that "the world will little note, nor long remember what we say here," but he was certainly accurate when he continued, saying, "but it can never forget what they did here."

In 1864 local citizens established the Gettysburg Battlefield Memorial Association to purchase and preserve key portions of the battlefield. Over the next three decades, thousands of visitors viewed the site and veterans held numerous reunions. In 1895 the association deeded its lands to the War Department to form the core of the Gettysburg National Military Park. By

1864

September 2
Sherman captures Atlanta.

November 8
Lincoln is reelected president.

November 15
Sherman begins the March to the Sea.

December 5–16
55,000 Union troops defeat Major General John Hood's army at Nashville.

December 21
Sherman reaches Savannah and the sea, leaving a swath of destruction in his wake.

the end of the century, dozens of monuments had been raised to honor units and individuals who had fought there, and the positions occupied by many of the units were marked. Military officers conducted "staff rides" to study the battle. In 1933

Crowds gathered for dedication of Soldiers National Cemetery on November 19, 1863.

the National Park Service assumed administration of the park. Today it is the most visited battlefield in North America and the focus of programs commemorating the Civil War and Abraham Lincoln.

Over the years land has been added to the park and work conducted to return its appearance to that of 1863. Commercial encroachment has been limited and facilities added to enhance visits to the battlefield and environs. In 1989 The Friends of Gettysburg was formed to raise funds to preserve the landscape and monuments of the battlefield. A decade later, in 1998, the Gettysburg National Battlefield Museum Foundation was established to raise funds to purchase lands for a buffer area to protect the battlefield from commercial encroachment, conserve the Gettysburg Cyclorama, and construct a museum and visitor center to place events at Gettysburg in historical perspective. The two organizations merged in 2006 to form the Gettysburg Foundation, realizing one of its major goals with the opening of the new Museum and Visitor Center at Gettysburg National Military Park in September 2008.

1865

January 31
The Thirteenth Amendment officially abolishes slavery.

March 25
Lee's forces in Petersburg attack Grant's army, and are defeated in four hours.

April 2
Lee evacuates Petersburg. Richmond is evacuated.

May
The C.S.A. reunites with the United States.

April 9
Lee surrenders to Grant at Appomattox.

April 14
John Wilkes Booth shoots Lincoln at Ford's Theatre in Washington. Lincoln dies the next morning at 7:22 a.m.

April 18
General Johnston surrenders to Sherman in North Carolina.

Key Participants

Officers of the Union

Brigadier General John Buford A career military officer, Buford returned from his post at Fort Crittenden, Utah, to serve the Union in 1861. He and his troops were the first Union soldiers to reach Gettysburg on June 30, when they encountered the Confederate column approaching the same area. Buford decided to stay in the area and camp overnight, essentially choosing Gettysburg as the field of the ensuing three-day battle.

Colonel Joshua L. Chamberlain Chamberlain left his quiet life as a Maine schoolteacher to fight for the Union, and eventually became commander of the Twentieth Maine Volunteer Infantry. At Gettysburg, the Twentieth Maine defended the high ground at Little Round Top from the Confederacy, ready to fight to the last man if necessary. When ammunition ran out, Chamberlain gave the extraordinary order to charge the enemy with bayonets drawn. The startled, exhausted Confederate soldiers retreated, giving the Union a major strategic victory.

Major General Winfield S. Hancock A career officer with distinguished service in the Mexican-American War, Hancock had already earned the nickname "Hancock the Superb" by the time he arrived at Gettysburg. Sent ahead by Major General George G. Meade on July 1, 1863, Hancock immediately took command of the Union's left wing, organizing forces on Cemetery Ridge and holding this position through three days of fighting. When he was wounded during Pickett's Charge, he refused evacuation and continued to command through the end of the battle. Hancock would go on to run for President of the United States in 1880.

Major General George G. Meade Early on the morning of July 28, 1863, a messenger arrived at Major General Meade's tent to inform him that President Lincoln had appointed him to replace Major General Joseph Hooker and take command of the Army of the Potomac. Meade, a career military officer and civil engineer, moved quickly to relocate the entire Army of the Potomac to Gettysburg on the night of July 1, creating a defensive line that proved impenetrable for the Confederacy. Meade received a promotion and a Thanks of Congress for his victory.

General John F. Reynolds Commander of I, III, and XI Corps, Reynolds had the unfortunate distinction of being the first and highest-ranking officer to die in battle at Gettysburg. Reynolds succumbed to a gunshot wound in the trees near McPherson Farm on the morning of July 1, 1863. With Reynolds's death, the Union forces were forced into a retreat through the town of Gettysburg and up into the high ground south of town, establishing the farmers' fields below and the surrounding ridges as pivotal battleground.

Major General Daniel E. Sickles A New York congressman, Sickles came to the war with his notoriety already established: He had gunned

down his wife's lover in the streets of Washington in broad daylight—and then received an acquittal from a sympathetic court. He formed his own brigade of 2,000 recruits, and rose through the ranks until he commanded the III Corps at Gettysburg. Meade placed Sickles's army on the left flank of the line early on July 2, but Sickles chose to abandon this land in favor of higher ground at the Peach Orchard. This move weakened the left flank and left the III Corps vulnerable.

Colonel Strong Vincent Considered one of the most promising officers in the Union army, Vincent commanded the Third Brigade, First Division of V Corps at Gettysburg, joining Chamberlain at Little Round Top and defending the brigade's right flank while Chamberlain fought at the left. It was Vincent who gave Chamberlain the order to hold the high ground at all costs. In the end, Vincent suffered the ultimate cost, receiving a gunshot wound to the thigh and groin that led to his death five days later.

Brigadier General Gouverneur K. Warren As chief engineer of the Army of the Potomac, Warren's survey of Little Round Top and the Union left flank contributed significantly to the Union victory on July 2. Seeing the strategically important hilltop standing undefended, Warren sent a staff member to find Union troops to occupy the hill. Thanks to Warren's quick thinking and initiative, Colonel Strong Vincent moved his brigade to Little Round Top, arriving just a few minutes before the Confederates charged the hill. The ensuing battle secured the hill as a Union stronghold.

Officers of the Confederacy

Brigadier General Lewis Armistead His hat placed on top of his sword point and hoisted high in the air, Armistead led his brigade of five Virginia regiments into Pickett's Charge, and this spontaneous gesture of valor became an enduring symbol of the battle. Armistead studied briefly at West Point, only to resign from the academy after breaking a plate over fellow cadet Jubal Early's head, but Armistead made his mark in battle in the Mexican-American War. At Gettysburg, Armistead was the officer who reached the Angle on July 3, making him the general who set the "high water mark" for the Confederacy's advance into Union territory.

Major General Jubal Early In the days before the battle at Gettysburg, Jubal Early seized the nearby town of York for the Confederacy and demanded a $28,000 ransom from the townspeople for its release (which he received). With this victory, Early had the distinction of taking the largest Northern town to fall to the Confederates during the war. Known to his friends and acquaintances as an eccentric, outspoken man with a tremendous vocabulary of profanity, Early had an early triumph at Gettysburg on July 1, when he and his troops defeated a division of the Union XI Corps on the Union's right flank, and drove them back through the city. On July 3, Early's men were part of the failed assault on Culp's Hill.

Lieutenant General Richard S. Ewell Wounded at Groveton in 1862, Richard Ewell lost his left leg below the knee but returned to battle some months later after a lengthy recovery. He was selected by General Stonewall Jackson to take over his own corps when Jackson was mortally wounded at Chancellorsville, and Ewell looked like the right choice when his brilliant strategy won the day for the Confederacy on July 1 at Gettysburg, capturing 4,000 men and twenty-three cannons and sending the Union XI and I Corps fleeing for the hills. When General Robert E. Lee sent orders to Ewell, however, to pursue the Union and take Cemetery Ridge "if practicable," Ewell held back. The result: The Union established its army on the high ground, acquiring a significant advantage over the Confederacy.

Major General Henry Heth A division commander in the Army of Northern Virginia, Heth was marching east from Cashtown, Pennsylvania, on July 1, when he sent two brigades ahead, apparently to perform reconnaissance (although his memoir suggests they were to look for shoes in Gettysburg). The brigades came upon Buford's Union cavalry north of Gettysburg, and they had little choice but to engage in battle—exactly what General Lee had ordered Heth not to do. Once engaged, the fighting intensified, and Heth found himself in combat against the Union's famous Iron Brigade. Heth was knocked unconscious, taking him out of battle for the next several days. Meanwhile, Confederate reinforcements arrived and forced the Union back through town and into the hills.

Lieutenant General A. P. Hill Hill had distinguished himself in battle at First Bull Run, Williamsburg, the Seven Days Battles, Antietam, Fredericksburg, and Chancellorsville, where he was wounded while commanding Stonewall Jackson's corps. At Gettysburg, Hill commanded the Confederate Third Corps of the Army of Northern Virginia, placing him at the head of most of the forces on July 2. Just before battle, he was known to put on a red hunting shirt, a garment his men called his "battle shirt" and saw as a warning to prepare arms for engagement.

Major General John Bell Hood Hood commanded a division of Major General James Longstreet's First Corps of the Army of Northern Virginia, which arrived at Gettysburg late on July 1. Lee's orders involved an assault on the Union's left flank the next day, but Hood's assignment led directly through Devil's Den, some of the rockiest and most dangerous ground in the entire Gettysburg topography. Hood protested to no avail, and at 4:00 p.m. on July 2, he led his troops around to the east, away from his assigned route, and attacked Little Round Top. Moments into the battle, Hood suffered a wound to his left arm that would cost him the use of it for the rest of his life.

General Robert E. Lee When the South seceded from the Union in 1861, Robert E. Lee made the difficult decision to leave his commission in the United States Army and join his fellow Virginians in defense of the new Confederate States of America. He served as a military advisor to C.S.A. President Jefferson Davis, who made him commander of the

Army of Northern Virginia in 1862. Fresh from a tremendous victory at Chancellorsville, but grieving over the loss in that battle of his greatest advisor, Thomas J. "Stonewall" Jackson, Lee came to Gettysburg with the plan of engaging the Union on their own ground and demoralizing the Federal army. Instead, he presided over a battle that would end with 51,000 men dead, wounded, or missing— and his army would never completely recover from the loss.

Lieutenant General James Longstreet Commander of the Army of Northern Virginia's First Corps, Longstreet earned the nickname "Old War Horse" from General Lee, who considered him his most trusted corps commander. At Gettysburg, however, Longstreet disagreed with Lee about the general's strategy, advocating for a defensive stance that would secure "good ground" between the Union army and Washington, DC. Lee insisted that they attack the Union's left flank on July 2, however, so Longstreet decided to wait for all of his forces to arrive before attacking—pushing the run on Little Round Top until 4:00 p.m. By the time Longstreet's men attacked, Little Round Top had a defensive force at its summit, and Confederate troops saw the heaviest and bloodiest fighting of the three-day battle at the Peach Orchard and Wheatfield. Longstreet's decision to delay this attack has been fodder for historical criticism ever since.

Major General George E. Pickett Pickett served the U.S. military during the Mexican-American War, on the Texas frontier and on the Pacific coast, then resigned from the U.S. Army and enlisted to serve his native Virginia. He was wounded at the Battle of Gaines' Mill, but rejoined the fighting in 1862, serving in defense near Richmond seeing little combat. The march to Gettysburg came as a welcome relief after so much inaction—but even at this monumental battle, Pickett's division stayed in the background during much of the fighting. On July 3, Pickett's still-fresh division became the natural choice to lead the battle that now bears his name: Pickett's Charge. More than 6,000 men were lost in the charge, but Pickett himself survived and lived to surrender in person at Appomattox.

Major General James Ewell Brown "J. E. B." Stuart An expert horseman, Stuart led the cavalry of the Army of Northern Virginia, a contingent that acted as General Lee's eyes and ears in the field. The exemplary war record of the deliberately ostentatious Stuart—who wore a red-lined cape and a peacock feather in his hat—included a flamboyant victory at Bull Run, and a legendary ride all the way around Union forces at Richmond, an act that humiliated the opposing army. Stuart's fortunes took a bad turn at Gettysburg, however, when he circled too far east and found himself 80 miles from Gettysburg, placing him out of contact with Lee and unable to warn him about the size, progress, and armament of the Union troops. "Well General, you are here at last," Lee noted when Stuart finally arrived in the Confederate camp on July 2—a strong rebuke from the rarely critical commander.

Gettysburg National Military Park: A Historical Tour

The best way to experience Gettysburg National Military Park is by spending at least one entire day here, allowing yourself to be transported back to July 1–3, 1863, by the museum, battlefield tour, and visits to historic sites in town. Plan to take whatever time you need to understand the troop maneuvers, the strategies of each commander, and the stories of soldiers who marched, fought, and lived or died on these pastoral farmers' fields and gently rolling hills. Imagine this landscape transformed by 163,000 men and more than 600 cannons, obscured by the gun-smoke haze hanging in the humid air.

New Facilities Help You Understand the Battle

Before you set off on the tour route, spend some time at the park museum and visitor center, where you can begin to grasp the enormity of the battle and the complex military decisions that succeeded or failed on this ground.

The **Museum and Visitor Center at Gettysburg National Military Park** provides invaluable perspective on the events that led up to the Battle at Get-

Begin your visit at the new Museum and Visitor Center.

From the viewing platform, visitors can enjoy the entire Cyclorama.

tysburg, the people who figured prominently in the battle, and the aftermath for the townspeople as well as the military. Plan to spend at least two to three hours at the visitor center, enough time to follow the sequence of events and their importance to each day of battle. The $12.50 admission charge ($11.50 for seniors and military, $8.50 for youth ages 6–18, free for children under age 6) includes all of the activities at the visitor center.

Before you plunge into the museum, start by seeing the film, *A New Birth of Freedom,* a brilliantly crafted twenty-two-minute overview of the battle and its significance to the Civil War. Narrated by Morgan Freeman, with Sam Waterston as the voice of Abraham Lincoln—delivering a definitive reading of the Gettysburg Address—the film provides a sense of the battle's drama, implications, and staggering size, using both historic and contemporary imagery to create a stirring synopsis of the events.

No trip to Gettysburg could be complete without seeing the meticulously restored **Battle of Gettysburg Cyclorama,** the famous 360-degree, 377-foot-long painting created in 1883 and 1884 by French master Paul Dominique Philippoteaux and a team of twenty artists. The park completed a five-year, $15 million restoration of this magnificent work in 2008, culminating in the painting's installation in a theater built for this purpose, within the visitor center. From a central viewing platform, visitors can see the painting's entire 42-foot height—12 feet of which were hidden in the old Cyclorama building—while a dramatic narrative tells the story of Pickett's Charge, and lighting, sound effects, and music bring the Cyclorama's story to life, placing you figuratively on Cemetery Ridge to view 22,000 soldiers involved in the fighting. The newly restored painting has never looked better or displayed more impressive detail.

Your Cyclorama experience may include a twenty- to thirty-minute wait in line before entering the theater; long escalators will take you up three stories to the viewing gallery (elevators are available for wheelchairs, strollers, and anyone needing assistance). At the end of the program, you will walk down a flight of stairs to the exit, where display cases contain a miniature version of the painting with annotations to help you identify the major characters.

The **Gettysburg Museum of the American Civil War** not only displays more than 300,000 artifacts from the Battle at Gettysburg, it also offers vast amounts of information about the battle, what preceded it, and what came after, bringing the park's wealth of information to visitors—some of it for the first time. Eleven galleries are organized around themes from Lincoln's Gettysburg Address, providing a context of ideals for which the Gettysburg Campaign and the war itself were fought. You'll learn what made Gettysburg a focal point for both armies, why this battle was important, what each side truly believed it was fighting for, and what happened on July 4 and after, when the troops marched away and left thousands of dead and dying men on farm fields owned by civilians. Multimedia presentations and interactive stations explain the reasons for the war and its progress before and after Gettysburg, while interpretive displays bring the war to a more personal level, describing the lives of soldiers on

The bookstore and country store at the Gettysburg Museum of the American Civil War offer a variety of gift items.

The Refreshment Saloon in the new visitor center offers hot meals, sandwiches, and ice cream.

Historical Tours

each side, the role of Gettysburg women in the battle, and the issues that made so many men enlist and fight for their rights or the rights of others.

Before you leave the visitor center, be sure to stop at the extensive Museum Bookstore and gift emporium, the country store (where you can buy locally made preserves and other edible goodies), and the Refreshment Saloon, where you can lunch on your favorite sandwiches and wraps or on Pennsylvania Dutch comfort-food specialties.

Extend your experience of the park with a visit to the **David Wills House** at 8 Lincoln Square in the town of Gettysburg. Renovated in 2009, this home became the center of activity for the monumental recovery operations after the 1863 battle—and in a second-floor bedroom, President Abraham Lincoln finished composing the Gettysburg Address. Open Dec–Feb, F–Su 10–5; Mar, Th–M 9–5; Apr, W–M 9–5; May–Aug, daily 9–6; Sep–Nov, W–M 9–5. Admission is $6.50 adults, $5.50 seniors, $4.00 youth 6–12, free to children 5 and under. (866) 486-5735, www.davidwillshouse.org.

The Days before the Battle

When Major General George Meade awakened abruptly in his tent near Frederick, Maryland, at 3:00 a.m. on June 28, 1863, he believed he was about to be arrested—while he'd committed no crime, political arrests were common among high-ranking officials and statesmen. The man who woke him, however, was Colonel James A. Hardie of the United States War Department, and he came with a critically important message: President Lincoln had named Meade the general in chief of the Army of the Potomac.

The appointment came after Lincoln's repeated orders to Major General Joseph Hooker, who was then general in chief, to advance against Confederate forces that had left the front near Fredericksburg to march into Maryland and Pennsylvania. Hooker's hesitation to act had resulted in a spectacular failure against Lee at Chancellorsville a few weeks before, a Confederate victory that bolstered Lee's confidence. Lee had begun a campaign to infiltrate Northern territory.

Meade had not sought the promotion and didn't care for the idea, but he was disgusted with Hooker's performance and understood the need to replace him. "I have been tried and condemned," he said of the surprise appointment, but his president had called him to duty, and he would serve his country with honor.

He had little information at that moment about Lee's whereabouts, but he and his advisors pieced together what they knew and determined that Lee was on his way north. Meade organized his troops to march toward Pennsylvania, search for the Confederate army, and establish a Northern defensive line.

Meanwhile, General Robert E. Lee and the Army of Northern Virginia had penetrated Union territory and entered Pennsylvania in the last week of June 1863. His men were gaunt from lack of adequate rations, the cost of Union victories in Virginia, Kentucky, and Tennessee that cut off supply lines and fed Federal troops with Confederate crops. Now in the Union's own land of plenty, the Confederate soldiers replenished their spent bodies with readily available fresh water, milk, butter, beef and pork, and ripe fruit from farmers' orchards.

Meeting little opposition as they advanced, the Army of Northern Virginia had made fairly easy progress, but Lee himself took no comfort in this. He

Southern Pennsylvania's peaceful existence would shatter as armies marched across Sachs Bridge near the soon-to-be battlefield at Gettysburg.

was used to regular reports of Union troop movements and activity from J. E. B. Stuart, head of Lee's cavalry and a sharp, daring intelligence officer. Stuart had not reported for days, however, and without information, Lee felt like a blind man leading his soldiers into hidden danger. He set a course for Harrisburg, Pennsylvania's capital, and planned to advance on this city in the next few days.

Lee moved forward with more conviction than he felt, until a new option came to him from one of his most trusted advisors, Lieutenant General James Longstreet. Longstreet had his own scout, Henry Thomas Harrison, who had brought him reliable, accurate information from the field on a regular basis for the last several months. Harrison reported that the Army of the Potomac was on its way north from Virginia in great numbers, signaling that a confrontation would soon be at hand in Pennsylvania. Worse, Harrison reported—erroneously—that the Union troops were following the exact route that Lee had taken, through the Appalachian Mountains. Not only did this mean that Lee's uncontested advance into the North would soon end, but his potential line of retreat was now blocked by oncoming Union troops.

Advance or retreat? Lee and his advisors examined the situation and chose a new course, putting aside their Harrisburg goal in favor of Gettysburg. The focal point in the middle of a network of roads connecting towns in Pennsylvania and Maryland, Gettysburg could become an important hub from which to block supplies and ammunition meant for the Union. Its access to the Chambersburg Pike and the roads to York and Baltimore made this small town of 5,000 people a strategic focus for both the Confederacy and the Federal army.

Lee sent messages to all of his forces to head for Gettysburg, but to avoid a general engagement until they could all reach this potential battleground. With his troops amassed, Lee knew that the Confederate army could take the town and triumph over the Union.

No Union ambush stopped the Army of Northern Virginia as troops entered southern Pennsylvania towns and stormed into shops, demanding to purchase food and supplies with Confederate script. While the money was worthless in the North, Lee had ordered his men to pay for what they took, and shopkeepers and farmers accepted the bills in hopes that they would someday be exchangeable for "real" money—and out of fear for their lives if they did not comply.

Civilian Life on the Edge of War

General Jubal Early and his men were the first Confederates to arrive in Gettysburg on Friday, June 26. Early's forces collided just outside of town with the Twenty-sixth Pennsylvania Emergency Cavalry, a volunteer squad that attempted an offensive strike and was roundly chased off—but not before Union Private George Washington Sandoe died of a bullet to the head. Sandoe, who had served in the army only for a few days, became the first casualty of the bloody battle that would follow in earnest several days later.

Gettysburg was left defenseless, the only Union protection already in retreat—and as townspeople realized that the Confederate army was approaching in earnest, they hurried to close their stores and prepare to defend their own homes. The local officials vacated the town the night before,

Local officials rushed to this train station on June 30, abandoning their constituents.

leaving residents with no formal leadership. Schools closed early, sending children home to be with their families. Many free African-Americans fled for the State Capitol in Harrisburg, dodging Southern troops who would take them back to slavery, while Gettysburg residents emptied their stores and shops and hid their goods in the mountains to keep from exchanging them for worthless Confederate paper.

The Stage Is Set

On the night of June 29, Lieutenant General A. P. Hill's Third Corps camped in Cashtown, 9 miles outside of Gettysburg. Major General Henry Heth ordered a brigade to Gettysburg on the morning of June 30 to search the town for supplies in the hope of acquiring shoes for his men, many of whom marched barefoot or in footwear so worn it barely held together. Just outside of Gettysburg, however, the brigade discovered a large Union cavalry force, with a major contingent of Federal infantry nearby. The Confederates turned around and headed back to Cashtown without entering Gettysburg, reporting their findings to Heth and to Lieutenant General A. P. Hill.

The Southern brigade's advance and retreat, however, did not escape the notice of Union Brigadier General John Buford, commander of the Union cavalry, who put the knowledge that Confederates had arrived at Gettysburg to work. By morning, he had gained definitive information about the enemy's whereabouts, and was prepared for the attack he knew would come shortly. He sent word to General John Reynolds that a battle was imminent, and asked that reinforcements arrive as quickly as possible.

In the Confederate camp at Cashtown, with their first real intelligence acquired about Union troop movements and standing orders from Lee to avoid confrontation until a critical mass of Confederate army divisions could arrive, the Southern troops prepared to approach Gettysburg the following day. Longstreet's corps camped 17 miles west of Gettysburg in Greenwood, while Lieutenant General Richard Ewell's three divisions were at Heidlersburg to the northeast and Green Village to the northwest. None of these forces were close enough to engage in battle early the next day, and they did not intend to do so.

Meade would not arrive at Gettysburg until 2:00 a.m. on July 2, but his infantry, cavalry, and artillery stood ready on June 30 for the onslaught to come.

Early on the morning of July 1, Meade was at his headquarters at Taney-town, Maryland, 12 miles southeast of Gettysburg. He expected to defend high ground there at Pipe Creek, just across the Maryland state line from Pennsylvania, and believed that the Confederate army was approaching that point.

Lee, meanwhile, had not reached Gettysburg either. He rode his horse alongside Longstreet on the Chambersburg Pike from Cashtown, placing him about 8 miles west of Gettysburg when the first shots were fired. He had given no new orders to engage in battle that morning.

Battlefield Etiquette: Respect Your National Military Park

Follow these basic rules during your visit to the Gettysburg battlefield:

- **Park only in designated areas.** Don't pull off the road onto grass or ground. Preservation efforts are underway throughout the park, including the sides of roadways, fields, and grassy areas.

- **Park on the right-hand side of the road only.** If all of the official parking spaces are taken at your tour stop, you are welcome to park on the road. Parking on the right side only will ensure a smooth flow of traffic along the tour route.

- **Remember that you are touring hallowed ground.** Enjoy your visit, but refrain from climbing on monuments or fences. Treat the park and its grounds with respect for the lives lost here, and for the magnitude of the events that took place in these peaceful farmers' fields, orchards, and woods.

Look for the park's Auto Tour signs.

Day 1

Tour Stop 1: McPherson's Ridge

The Union Stops the Confederates' First Advance

You are standing in McPherson's Farm, where the first shots of the Battle of Gettysburg were fired. To the north, you can see Chambersburg Pike, the road Lee and Longstreet took to arrive in Gettysburg. The white barn before you and to the right is one of several original structures that remain on the battlefield. To your right (east) is Seminary Ridge, and you can see the Lutheran Theological Seminary to the southeast. These landmarks will come into play later on Day 1.

At 5:30 a.m. on July 1, a column of Confederate infantry under Henry Heth was on its way here

On the morning of July 1, McPherson's barn stood at the rear of the Union line.

from its campsite in Cashtown. They intended to obey Lee's orders to avoid confrontation until all Confederate troops were assembled, but Brigadier General John Buford, leader of the Union cavalry, took positions on McPherson's Ridge, to your right, to prepare for battle. As the Confederates came over Herr's Ridge and moved into range, Union Lieutenant Marcellus Jones fired the first shot at about 7:30 a.m. Planned or not, the Rebel infantry had engaged the Union.

When Confederate forces approaching Gettysburg heard gunfire, troops ran to the scene, joining their fellow soldiers and quickly outnumbering Buford's men. Buford knew he had to force the Confederates to remain west of Gettysburg until General John Reynolds arrived with his division . . . and at about 9:45 a.m., Buford spotted Reynolds galloping ahead of his corps. In minutes, Reynolds sent in his I Corps and urged the XI Corps to follow.

By 10:30, as Confederates were entering the woods to your left, the Union's famous, hard-charging Iron Brigade arrived. Instantly, they engaged the men commanded by Brigadier General James Jay Archer, who came at them with guns blazing. Seeing his men falling before the Confederate volley, Reynolds rode forward to encourage them—and when he looked back to see if reinforcements were coming, a bullet pierced his neck. He fell from his horse and died on the spot, the first and highest-ranking officer to die in the Battle at Gettysburg. A marker in front of the woods now indicates the spot where Reynolds fell.

Meanwhile, to the northwest and on the Union right, two Southern regiments—the Second and

"I will fight them inch by inch, and if driven into the town I will barricade the streets and hold them as long as possible."

—General John Reynolds in a message to Major General George Meade, July 1, 1863

General John Reynolds fell and perished on this spot.

This memorial to Reynolds stands at McPherson's Ridge.

Forty-second Mississippi—mistook an unfinished railroad cut (now the railroad right-of-way to your right) for a safe haven and leaped into it, thinking that this would provide some shelter from gunfire. They realized their error immediately when they saw that the sides of the cut were too steep to climb— they were trapped. They eagerly surrendered to the Union brigade above them. The 225 captured men and seven officers were now prisoners of war.

Back on the Union's left flank, the Twenty-fourth Michigan of the Iron Brigade found Archer's troops exposed and in rough ground across Willoughby Run, along the western border of McPherson's Farm (to your left). Circling the Confederates' right flank, they attacked the Southern troops from the rear while the Nineteenth Indiana, seeing the opportunity, attacked them head-on. By the end of the battle at 11:30 a.m., the Iron Brigade had captured Archer and seventy-five of his men, marching them to the rear of the Union lines, or right in front of you as you face McPherson's Farm. Here took place one of the most quoted exchanges in the entire battle. Archer, a prisoner and in disgrace, suddenly ran into his old friend Major General Abner Doubleday, commander of the Union's I Corps. Doubleday greeted his friend warmly, saying, "Good morning, Archer, how are you? I'm glad to see you!"

Archer, not in the mood for reunions, replied curtly, "Well, I'm not glad to see you by a damn sight!"

As the battle came to a close and each side retreated from the field to assess and reorganize, an elderly gentleman with a rifle walked up to the Union commanders. John Burns, Gettysburg's 69-year-old former town constable, came to volunteer with the Union army and fight for the United States. Burns was the only man in Gettysburg who joined the fighting—and for his courage he was wounded later that day. Happily, his wound was not fatal, and he lived several more years beyond the battle.

Union brigades held this position near McPherson's Farm until 11:30 a.m., as indicated by numerous monuments to their bravery.

John Burns was the only civilian from Gettysburg to volunteer in the army.

Tour Stop 2: Eternal Light Peace Memorial/Oak Hill

A Noble Assault Goes Terribly Wrong

You've come to Oak Hill, the site of one of the most ill-fated battles of the Gettysburg campaign. The Eternal Light Peace Memorial has graced this hill since July 3, 1938—the seventy-fifth anniversary of the battle—when 200,000 people, including many Civil War veterans in their 90s, came to see President Franklin Delano Roosevelt dedicate the monument. Oak Hill is a high point west and northwest of town, one that represented an important strategic conquest for the army that succeeded in reaching and securing it.

At 2:30 p.m. on July 1, 1863, Confederates who had just arrived at Gettysburg emerged from the woods here, looked across the Mummasburg Road, and saw what seemed to be the right end of the Union I Corps. Major General Robert Rodes

More than 200,000 people attended the 1938 dedication of the Eternal Light Peace Memorial.

ordered his three brigades—some 8,000 men—to attack I Corps, but instead of choosing his most qualified commanders to lead the charge, he chose Brigadier General Edward A. O'Neal and Colonel Alfred J. Iverson Jr., two comparatively inexperienced commanders. The idea was to attack the left, right, and center of the Union corps' line, forcing them to retreat or surrender.

But when O'Neal attacked at the wrong time and place, Rodes may have realized his error; and when Iverson's men started to veer to the left before his eyes, Rodes could do nothing to correct the problem. Iverson's brigade headed for a stone wall, a perfect hiding place for the Union I Corps—and sure enough, when the Southern brigade came within range, the Union rose up and rained musket shot on them, killing or wounding nearly all of them. The few survivors among the 900 men managed to raise white handkerchiefs to surrender.

At the end of the day, O'Neal's recent promotion was rescinded, and Iverson was removed from command.

Iverson's men approached this stone wall on Oak Hill, where an ambush awaited them.

Tour Stop 3: Oak Ridge

The Union Line Crumbles

July 1 started off as a good day for the Union, with a morning's victory against an army engaged in battle sooner than expected, and Confederate military might scattered across the countryside. That was before the much-maligned Union XI Corps, under Major General Oliver Howard, spread out across the field near Oak Ridge, where you're standing.

Primarily composed of German-born immigrants, the XI Corps had suffered a humiliating defeat at Chancellorsville just a few weeks before, when they had actually run from the field of battle

Union soldiers died by the hundreds on Day 1 of the battle.

when General Stonewall Jackson attacked them. As a result, they became the brunt of jokes passed throughout the Army of the Potomac, who labeled them with nicknames including "Howard's Cowards" and the "Flying Dutchmen."

Eager to redeem his good name and his soldiers' reputations, Howard took command of the field when Reynolds was killed, placing Brigadier General Carl Schurz in command of the XI Corps, much of which had not yet arrived on the field of battle. As the three divisions of the XI Corps appeared, they deployed to the north of town at Oak Hill, with one division placed in reserve at Cemetery Hill. (You can see the hill southeast of here, on the other side of the town of Gettysburg.) Finding Oak Hill already occupied by Confederates, the division led by Brigadier General Francis Barlow took higher ground directly behind you at

See the whole battlefield— including McLean's barn—from Oak Ridge.

From the ridge, soldiers had a wide view of the Gettysburg valley and approaching troops.

"Up and down the line men reeling and falling, splinters flying from wheels and axles where bullets hit; in the rear, horses tearing and plunging . . . bullets hissing, humming, and whistling everywhere; cannon roaring . . . smoke, dust, splinters, blood; wreck and carnage indescribable . . ."

Augustus Buell, Union cannoneer, July 1, 1863

Blocher's Knoll (more on this in a moment), while Brigadier General Alexander Schimmelfennig's division moved several hundred yards to the north.

The result of this shuffling proved disastrous for XI Corps. With Barlow up on Blocher's Knoll, the left flank of the corps' line formed an angle to the I Corps' right, leaving the XI's right flank undefended. Confederates streamed in from the north and took down Barlow's division in short order, and when Schimmelfennig's division rushed to cover Barlow, the Confederates demolished their ranks. The remaining third division raced down from Cemetery Hill to attempt to stem the Confederate advance, but it fell as well . . . and the men of the XI Corps retreated with haste through the streets of Gettysburg, repeating their unfortunate history and sealing their reputation as the weakest corps in the Union army. They finally regrouped well south of town on top of Cemetery Hill, and remained there until the Union marched out several days later.

At the same time, here on Oak Ridge, the Confederates also attacked the Union I Corps. Union Junior General John Robinson ordered Colonel James W. Tilden of the Sixteenth Maine to "take that position and hold it at any cost," and Tilden and his 298 men did so, knowing full well that their small numbers could not hold the ridge for long against entire Confederate divisions. At the last moment, with the day clearly lost, Tilden lifted his sword high and plunged it into the ground, breaking it off at the hilt so that no Confederate could capture it and use it against a Union soldier. Turning to his men for their assistance, he took down their Maine flag, and together they tore it into many sections, each taking a piece of tattered fabric. Each man would carry pieces of their banner into Confederate POW prisons all over the South, keeping it as a reminder of the courage their leader had shown in his final hour.

Several of these men retained their fragments of the flag long after the war. You can view some of these in the Gettysburg battlefield visitor center.

Climb the Observation Tower for a panoramic view of the land surrounding Gettysburg and the preserved first day's battlefield. The red barn at the base of the valley is part of the McLean Farm, one of several structures that became a holding site for prisoners of war. Gettysburg College is to your right, while the town of Gettysburg stretches along the horizon in front of you and to the right as well.

A red-tailed hawk joins the eagle atop this monument to I Corps' Eighty-third New York Infantry.

Tour Stop 3A: Barlow Knoll

The Union's Right Flank

This stop is not marked with an Auto Tour Stop sign. You'll come to Barlow Knoll as you follow the tour route and proceed up Howard Avenue.

Here at this high point to the north of Gettysburg, Brigadier General Francis Barlow's division of XI Corps formed the extreme right end of the Union line. Barlow and his men defended this high ground, knowing that it was vulnerable to attack from many directions. For Barlow's bravery, history has renamed this spot Barlow Knoll—but the victory did not go to Barlow.

Barlow Knoll was a distant target, well to the east of Oak Ridge.

At 3:30 p.m. on July 1, 1,800 Confederate soldiers poured over the hill, whooping and hollering in the style that the Union called "rebel yells." They came at Barlow from every side, smashing the Union corps and sending them scrambling for safety. In minutes, the entire Union line began to crumble.

By about 4:00 p.m., as the Union retreated through town and the Confederate army gave chase, General Lee finally arrived in Gettysburg and had the satisfaction of seeing that his men had the opposing army on the run. His pleasure was short-lived, however: From his high position on Seminary Ridge, he could see the Union regrouping at Cemetery Hill and taking high ground with no opposition. Lee gave the order to General R. S. Ewell to attack them: "Take that hill, if practicable."

Brigadier General Francis Barlow defended and lost this ground, on which his memorial stands, to Confederate attack.

Ewell was not at all certain that it was practicable. He hesitated, weighing his corps' fatigue at the end of a long day of battle against the forces amassing on the other side of town. In the end, he did not attack—and this decision allowed the Union to bring in reinforcements, deploy their artillery and form the defensive line that would prove so hard to penetrate the next day. Despite the Union's severe losses on July 1, Cemetery Hill became a focal point in the progression of the battle, one that swung the advantage to the Union.

Walk to the top of the knoll, and see the excellent view of Gettysburg and the battlefield from its height. Interpretive signs provide a concise description of the battle.

Tour Stop 3B: Lutheran Theological Seminary

Medical Care for Every Soldier, Regardless of Uniform

This stop does not have an Auto Tour stop sign, but you will pass it as you proceed along Seminary Avenue and cross Chambersburg Road.

This is the Lutheran Theological Seminary, which became both a battleground and a field hospital on July 1. Field medics, local physicians, and Gettysburg residents treated both Union and Confederate wounded here until late September 1863, nearly three months after the battle. The main building is on your left.

"I have been operating all day long and have got the chief part of the butchering done in a satisfactory manner," Union Captain John Shaw Billings, a surgeon with the Second Division, I Corps, wrote to his wife. "I am utterly exhausted mentally and physically, having been operating night and day and am still hard at work. I have been left here in charge of 700 wounded with no supplies and have my hands full. Our division lost terribly."

Sometime after 3:00 p.m., the Union's I Corps attempted a last stand here on Seminary Ridge, turning to face what they expected would be the same army they had fought all afternoon. To their surprise, a division of fresh Confederate troops swooped in and quickly scattered their ranks, driving them through the streets of Gettysburg. I Corps soon joined XI Corps on Cemetery Hill.

By this time, you're certainly wondering where General Meade was and when he arrived at Gettysburg. With no mass communication and his headquarters 12 miles away from the fighting, Meade did not know that the battle had begun until about noon on July 1. He found out when a newspaper reporter came to his headquarters in Taneytown, Maryland, and asked to use his telegraph to send his coverage of the battle to his editor! Meade immediately sent Major General Hancock to Gettysburg, and began sending orders to the Union's corps in the area to converge on Gettysburg. By morning, the Union's complement was 60,000 soldiers—while the Confederacy built its forces overnight as well, bringing the Confederate army at Gettysburg up to 50,000 men. Meade himself left Taneytown about 10:00 p.m. and arrived in Gettysburg at midnight to begin his inspection and extension of the Union line.

Lutheran Theological Seminary became a field hospital for both armies during and after the battle.

Historical Tours

Day 2

Tour Stop 4: North Carolina Memorial

The Confederate Line

Between the Lutheran Seminary and Warfield Ridge (Tour Stop 7), you're following the Confederate line. You've passed through McMillan Woods, and you can now see to your left the field of battle much as Lee and his men saw it on July 2.

More than 600 big guns—cannons and other major artillery—were positioned along this line. About 400 of these are still in the park, many of them carefully preserved to look as they did on the day of battle.

Imagine a long line of soldiers in blue uniforms across the fields, some 85,000 strong by mid-afternoon on July 2, extending beyond the horizon in both directions—while at the same time, the Confederate army had about 75,000 men, spread along the ridgeline on which you are standing. The Union line stretched from Cemetery Ridge—to

More than 600 big guns were stationed along the Confederate line.

your far right as you face the battlefield—all the way to Culp's Hill, straight across from you behind Cemetery Hill. Meade positioned the 3½-mile line on the high ground from end to end, so that it curled around back on itself at Culp's Hill, creating a large fishhook. In contrast, the Confederate army would cross rocky, boulder-strewn ground and hundreds of yards of wide-open farmland to reach the Union position.

Why was the fishhook important? The overlapping "barb" of the hook around Culp's Hill formed a short interior line, allowing Meade to bring men, guns, and supplies from that area to anywhere along his entire line from behind. With a shorter distance to travel and the advantage of moving without full exposure to Confederate fire, the men and guns could fill a gap in the line or reinforce an area of heavy fighting with efficiency. This made the Union army particularly formidable in the heat of battle.

Soldiers of North Carolina guard their colors in this striking monument, designed by Mount Rushmore sculptor Gutzon Borglum.

Tour Stop 5: Virginia Memorial

A Disagreement on Strategy

General Robert E. Lee

"General Lee never in his life gave me orders to open an attack at a specific hour. He was perfectly satisfied that when I had my troops in position and was ordered to attack, no time was ever lost. On the night of the 1st I left him without any orders at all. On the morning of the 2d I went to General Lee's head-quarters at daylight and renewed my views against making an attack. He seemed resolved, however, and we discussed the probable results."

—**Lieutenant General James Longstreet, in a memoir compiled by his daughter, Helen Longstreet, 1904**

On the morning on July 2, a strange quiet settled over the battlefield. At the first light of day, Lee and Longstreet, conferring at Lee's headquarters in a farmhouse on Chambersburg Pike, had disagreed on the strategy most appropriate for Confederate victory: Longstreet advocated a move around the Union's left flank, placing the Army of Northern Virginia between the Union's Army of the Potomac—virtually all of which was now spread before them—and the Federal capital in Washington, DC. This would force Meade to attack the Confederate army at its strongest, Longstreet argued, and the Confederacy would continue to hold the advantage it had gained in Chancellorsville.

Lee found many flaws in Longstreet's strategy. The general in chief noted that if the Confederate army chose to withdraw now, it would be vulnerable to an offensive strike by the Union while the Southern corps made their move. With so much armament and wagons full of supplies, Lee was certain that Longstreet overestimated their ability to move swiftly and decisively. In the end, Lee told Longstreet, "If Meade is there tomorrow, I will attack him."

Still lacking the real information he needed from his cavalry officer, J. E. B. Stuart, Lee confirmed his orders for Longstreet and Ewell. Lee believed that the Union left flank was in the Peach Orchard—when it was actually on high ground on Cemetery Ridge, well east of the orchard. He directed Longstreet to proceed up Emmitsburg

Road to attack Meade's left flank, while Ewell, at the same time, would attack the Union's right flank at Cemetery Hill and Culp's Hill. With both flanks under attack, A. P. Hill's division would go after the Union center, keeping the Union occupied until the Confederate backup arrived: a fresh division led by Major General Richard Anderson. The simultaneous strike would roll up both ends of the Union line, forcing them toward the center and the arriving fresh corps. Lee ordered the simultaneous attack for dawn on July 2.

It was a good plan, but Lee's lack of real intelligence about the Union line, coupled with a controversial decision by Longstreet, would lead the Confederate army into one of the bloodiest battles of the entire war.

From the Virginia Memorial, the battleground stretches before the Confederate line.

Tour Stop 6: Pitzer Woods

Longstreet's Delay and Barksdale's Charge

The bloodiest day of fighting began here, but not until very late in the day—for a number of reasons that have been debated by the participants, military experts, and Civil War historians for more than 150 years.

With their orders in place, Ewell's men waited in the early morning drizzle at the Confederate left flank to make the attack on the Union's right. Longstreet's men, however, were still in transit to Gettysburg, with two divisions several miles away from the field and traveling through the morning hours. It was after 8:00 a.m. when they arrived, making Lee's original plan for a dawn attack impossible.

Lee regrouped and ordered Longstreet's men to begin moving in the mid-morning. Two divisions began as the sky cleared, but well into the march, their scouts informed them of a ridge they did not know was there—one that would put them in full

From Pitzer Woods, Little Round Top is in full view to the southeast.

view of Union troops on Little Round Top. The two divisions, a total of 16,000 men, now had to backtrack along the dusty Emmitsburg Road and take a more hidden route through the woods to the end of Seminary Ridge, or about where you are standing now. It was 3:30 p.m. before the men were in position to attack the Union's left flank.

Meanwhile, on the Union line, Major General Daniel Sickles believed his III Corp was in a position of disadvantage: They'd found themselves in low ground at Chancellorsville and took a terrible beating from the Confederates there, and Sickles was determined not to allow this to happen again. Now, stationed on the south end of Cemetery Ridge near Little Round Top, he looked toward the high ground along Emmitsburg Road directly in front of him, and decided it was a better position than the one he'd been ordered to hold. Sickles moved swiftly to defend this high ground, leaving his position on Cemetery Ridge and opening a gap in the Union's defensive line. His new position created a salient, or angle, which proved within hours to be a drastic error.

At long last, Longstreet's men loaded their cannons and opened fire on the Peach Orchard and Devil's Den (in front of you, slightly to the right) at 4:00 p.m. Ewell's men, who intended to hit the Union's right flank at the same time as Longstreet's charge, did not advance on Culp's Hill until 7:00 p.m., three hours after Longstreet's attack. We'll learn more about Ewell's attack when we reach Tour Stop 13.

You see the monument here for Brigadier General William Barksdale's Mississippi Brigade, on the spot on which Barksdale stood, waiting to join the

The State of Louisiana Memorial stands at Pitzer Woods, recognizing its men who fought at Culp's Hill and Cemetery Hill.

Historical Tours

attack. Barksdale was frustrated by the delays and kept asking for orders to advance; but the orders did not come until just after 6:00 p.m. So primed for combat was Barksdale's Brigade that they charged headlong into the battle at the Peach Orchard and Sherfy Farm (in front of you), with Barksdale leading the charge on horseback. Brigadier General William T. Wofford's Georgia Brigade followed on his heels, overtaking the Union's Ninth Massachusetts Battery and First Battery in the Wheatfield. The force and momentum of the Confederate brigades overwhelmed the exhausted Union army, and in no time the Federal line collapsed. From here, Barksdale spotted the gap in the Union line between Cemetery Ridge and Little Round Top—the gap left by Sickles's corps, which now fought for their lives in the Peach Orchard and Wheatfield—and rushed to penetrate the Union line.

Even with all the ground they had gained and the zeal with which they fought, the Confederate attack suddenly lost momentum as it reached the area around Plum Run, east of the Peach Orchard. In a last-ditch rally, the Union army drove the Mississippians back. Barksdale tried to regain the advantage, but a marksman's bullet reached him and took him out of the battle. He died later that night in a Union field hospital.

From the observation tower just after the intersection, you'll have an excellent view of the July 2 battlefield, including Sherfy Farm spreading directly before you to the east, Trostle Farm beyond that, and Spangler Farm to the northeast. Behind you, Eisenhower Farm—home of our thirty-fourth President, Dwight David Eisenhower—stretches to the west and south.

Tour Stop 7: Warfield Ridge

···

The Extreme Right End of the Confederate Line

Big Round Top (right) and Little Round Top were clear targets to Longstreet from Warfield Ridge, west of the two hills.

Longstreet's Fifteenth Alabama Brigade attacked from here at 4:00 p.m. Once the advance began, Colonel William C. Oates led the Forty-seventh Alabama Regiment to "pass up between the Round Tops, find the Union left, turn it and capture Little Round Top." Reinforcing Longstreet's attack was Major General John B. Hood's Confederate Division, on Longstreet's right.

What the 16,000 Confederate soldiers who emerged from the woods hadn't counted on, however, was a volley of gunfire from the green-uniformed crackerjack snipers of an elite Union regiment known as Berdan's Sharpshooters. Brigadier General Hiram Berdan commanded the First United States Sharpshooters, a regiment he had conceived and assembled shortly after the war began at Fort Sumter. The one major requirement, according to announcements distributed as the company was formed, was this: "No man would be enlisted who could not put ten bullets in succession within five inches from the center at a distance of six hundred feet from a rest or three hundred feet off hand."

On July 2, four companies of sharpshooters shot an average of ninety-five rounds per man. Confederates in command against them believed that the 300 men in the company who fired on them (100 sharpshooters and 200 men of the Third Maine, firing with muskets) were actually ten times as many men.

Despite the sharpshooters' skills, however, the Fifteenth Alabama eventually prevailed, and headed for Little Round Top.

On your way to Tour Stop 8, stop and take the trail to the top of Big Round Top. No fighting took place on this hill, but it offers a spectacular view of the battlefield and surrounding area.

Tour Stop 8: Little Round Top

The Union Turns the Tide of Battle

Plan to leave your vehicle at this tour stop and walk along the paved paths at the top of Little Round Top. Some of Gettysburg's most memorable and heroic moments took place here.

When the Texas and Alabama Brigades under Hood attacked here, shortly after 4:00 p.m., they had no way of knowing that there was no Union army on the summit. Under orders from General Meade, Brigadier General John Geary had moved his division of the XII Corps to Culp's Hill, at the northern end of the Union line. Sickles had moved his troops—without orders—to the high ground near the Peach Orchard, leaving this strategically critical hill undefended. Little Round Top would have fallen to the Confederates in short order, had it not been for one man's foresight and quick thinking.

Brigadier General Gouverneur K. Warren, chief engineer of the Army of the Potomac, was sent to this hill by General Meade to check on the "peppering"—the sound of cannon fire from the woods. To Warren's amazement, he arrived and found the hill unmanned. Peering into the woods with his binoculars, he saw the glint of sunlight against polished metal, and knew that this must mean artillery in the forest. He knew immediately that the loss of this hilltop could mean disaster for the Union army.

Warren sent messengers in all four directions to call regiments to occupy this high ground and face the approaching onslaught. This action earned

"But for the timely advance of the V Corps and the prompt sending of a portion to Round Top, where they met the enemy almost on the crest and had a desperate fight to secure the position—I say but for these circumstances the enemy would have secured Round Top and planted his artillery there, commanding the whole battlefield, and what the result would have been I leave to you to judge."

—General George Meade

Historical Tours

Brigadier General Gouverneur K. Warren

Brigadier General Warren and his staff at Gettysburg

Warren the nickname "Hero of Little Round Top," and his statue here portrays him with binoculars in hand, forever surveying the hill he protected.

Colonel Strong Vincent was the first to respond to Warren's urgent message, bringing his brigade of 1,300 men—the Eighty-third Pennsylvania, Forty-fourth New York, Sixteenth Michigan, and Twentieth Maine—and assembling quickly on the hilltop, just ten minutes before the Fifteenth Alabama Brigade and the fearsome Texas Brigade arrived.

Hood's Texans and Alabamans stormed the hill, coming out of the woods at the base of Little Round Top. Vincent's men drove them back, but they came again . . . and in this second assault, Vincent was shot. He died five days later in a field hospital.

Closely following Vincent's men were Captain Augustus Martin and Lieutenant Charles Hazlett of the V Corps artillery brigade, lugging their big guns

inch by inch up the steep slope. Hazlett would also perish in one of the many assaults by the Alabama and Texas brigades, who rushed the hill over and over again and inflicted many casualties, only to be beaten back by the Union regiments at the top.

From Devil's Den, Little Round Top proved a tough fight for the Confederates.

53

Just as the Union solders thought their fight was lost, Colonel Patrick O'Rorke of the 140th New York Infantry led his 540 men over the hill from behind Little Round Top. Charging right down Little Round Top without stopping, the New Yorkers startled the Southern regiments and drove them back down the hill. O'Rorke himself took musket fire and died on the battlefield.

After three hours of fighting, with leaders succumbing to rifle fire and their own ammunition running low, the Twentieth Maine, under Colonel Joshua Chamberlain, realized that their orders to fight here "despite all hazards" might indeed lead

The Twentieth Maine Monument honors one of the most famous regiments in the Gettysburg campaign.

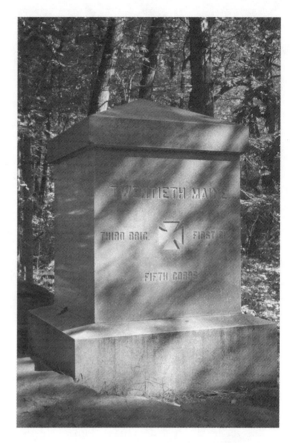

to every man's death. Seeing his left flank beginning to crumble, Chamberlain gave the inventive order to his men to fix bayonets and charge headlong into the Southern assault. The shocked Confederate soldiers, worn out from rushing uphill over and over again, saw the steel points coming at them and lost their nerve, swiftly retreating back across the open field to Devil's Den and the woods. Chamberlain's courageous move ended the assault on his side of the hill, earning him the Congressional Medal of Honor for this maneuver.

Walk to the top of the hill, where you'll find an

excellent view and many memorials, including one of the most famous and photographed memorials in the park: the castle, a tribute to the men of the Forty-fourth and Twelfth New York Infantry, who fought at Little Round Top and in many other battles throughout the three days.

Look to the valley below. Down and a little to

The Forty-fourth New York Infantry Monument is one of the park's most unusual structures.

Federals constructed breastworks hastily on Little Round
Top.

the left is Devil's Den, a rocky patch of ground that proved to be a deadly trap for both Union and Confederate forces. The Southern army placed sharpshooters here to pick off officers and men at the top of Little Round Top, which they did with considerable success. Both armies fought to gain this land, but it was Hood's division, temporarily under the command of General Evander Law, that slugged it out with the 124th New York and the Ward's Brigade—some 2,200 men—holding Devil's Den at the end of the day. Law's quick ascent to command when Hood fell to an exploding artillery shell earlier in the day triggered some of the chaos that ensued throughout the afternoon and early evening, and Law has been roundly criticized by modern historians—but by hook or by crook, he secured a small Confederate victory on this rocky ground.

Before you to the right are the Peach Orchard and the Wheatfield, two areas in which the heaviest and most deadly fighting took place on July 2. We'll learn more about the battle there in our next tour stop.

Tour Stop 9: The Wheatfield

The Bloody Field of War

You've reached the site of some of the most jumbled and confusing fighting in the entire battle at Gettysburg—so bewildering that many historians describe the massive confrontation here as a "whirlpool" of battle. The nodding stalks of golden wheat that thrived on these twenty acres of John Rose's farm on July 2, 1863, became a trampled mass in the space of two and a half hours, covered with blood and with the bodies of wounded, dying, and dead men. By the end of the day, more than 4,600 men had been killed or wounded or had gone missing in this little field, where 9,000 men had converged as one regiment after another was drawn into the vortex of battle.

The placid Wheatfield became one of the bloodiest killing grounds of the war.

Historical Tours

This Confederate soldier was one of hundreds who lost their lives at Devil's Den.

Sickles's insistence on disobeying orders and moving his men to the high ground at the Peach Orchard essentially forced his division to fight on the boulder-strewn Devil's Den and in Rose's Woods, the tree-congested land just beyond the field. Regiments from New York, Indiana, and Pennsylvania completed the ranks that stretched from Devil's Den through Rose's Woods to the Wheatfield, while Colonel Philip Regis de Trobriand's Third Brigade of the First Division of III Corps—five regiments from Maine, Michigan, New York, and Pennsylvania—covered the woods west of the Wheatfield. The Eighth New Jersey under Colonel John Ramsey would join them there.

The battle began in earnest at 4:30 p.m. when Confederate Brigadier General Jerome Robertson

moved his men of Hood's Division to attack Union troops at Devil's Den. Brigadier General Henry Benning's brigade followed closely after Robertson's men, and by 5:45 p.m., the rest of Hood's division under Brigadier General George Anderson moved to attack de Trobriand's men in the Wheatfield.

As the fighting grew intense, the V Corps arrived to cover de Trobriand's right flank. Longstreet's second division, commanded by Major General Lafayette McLaws, entered the battle at about 6:00 p.m., soon contributing to the overwhelming force on de Trobriand's men. By the time the Union II Corps arrived from Cemetery Ridge, de Trobriand had begun to withdraw and other brigades found themselves surrounded by Confederate troops. The battle pushed toward the Peach

Devil's Den today is a peaceful, carefully maintained area for contemplation of the dramatic events that took place here.

Orchard, with the Union making its stand there at 6:15 p.m.

When the carnage finally ended, the advantage had changed six times. In the end, the Confederates held the land, planting their flag in Devil's Den, but the slaughter extracted a heavy toll on both sides, tempering the sense of victory for the Southern army and deepening the Union's defeat.

Once the fighting ended, a conundrum of horror remained on the field of war: Neither side could transport the bodies of the wounded and dead from this open field, as any attempt to do so would endanger even more lives. The remaining men of the severely depleted Union and Confederate armies retreated into their ranks, leaving their comrades lying in the Wheatfield. Days passed before medical help arrived.

Of the hundreds of personal stories told in soldiers' journals, one of the most courageous and poignant involved Colonel Harrison Jeffords of the Fourth Michigan. In the midst of frenzied battle, Jeffords saw the Union flag fall to the ground and a Confederate soldier reaching for the flagpole. Jeffords instantly shot the Southern soldier and was about to lunge for the pole himself, but another Rebel saw him and thrust his bayonet into Jeffords— and then died as well, shot by one of Jeffords' men. Jeffords saved his country's flag but lost his life on the battlefield, calling for his mother with his dying breath. He was 26 years old.

Tour Stop 10: The Peach Orchard

The Union Salient

Here in the Peach Orchard, Sickles's division formed a salient—a place in the Union line that came to a point, instead of continuing in the tight, straight line Meade had ordered all corps to form across the countryside. Sickles's unauthorized move here from Cemetery Ridge put the commander and his men in a position in which they could be attacked from more than one side, making them particularly vulnerable to Confederate forces.

The Peach Orchard battle still intrigued artists of Keystone View Company, who made steropticon slides—a popular form of entertainment—in 1900.

A marker on Trostle Farm
stands where Sickles fell.

So they stood at 5:30 p.m., when Brigadier General J. B. Kershaw of McLaws's division attacked the men of Sickles's III Corps here in the Peach Orchard. The Confederates fell before the heavy fire from thirty Union cannons, but at 6:00 p.m., Barksdale and Wofford's brigades attacked from the west, jarring the nerves of the beleaguered Union troops with their whooping rebel yells. Sickles's men continued to fight bravely, but the two fresh Confederate brigades drove them back toward their original position at Cemetery Ridge. Sickles was defeated in short order, and half of his men died in the battle.

Over the years since 1863, the original peach trees were removed from this former orchard. Gettysburg National Military Park has engaged in a restoration process to bring all of the battlefield

areas back to their 1863 appearance, replant-
ing the Peach Orchard with actual peach trees to
provide visitors with a more authentic experience
of the battleground.

Seen here from Pitzer's Woods,
the Peach Orchard has been
replanted by the park.

As you drive between Tour Stops 10 and 11,
you'll pass the Abraham Trostle Farm. Sickles
used this farmhouse as his headquarters between
battles—and the diamond-shaped marker in the
yard indicates the spot where a Confederate
bullet found Sickles, shattering his leg. Ever the
blustering commander, Sickles continued to issue
orders even as his men carried him off the battlefield on a stretcher—and while he lost most of his
leg, he survived to return to public life. In fact, it
was Congressman Sickles who sponsored the
bill to preserve Gettysburg as a National Military
Park.

Tour Stop 11: Plum Run

The Valley of Death

A creek called Plum Run borders the field known by Gettysburg soldiers and historians as the Valley of Death. This no man's land between the Union and Confederate lines is where many of the wounded managed to crawl from the Wheatfield, but they could not cross Plum Run . . . so these wounded men lay in this valley until July 4, when the Battle at Gettysburg came to an end and medical help could finally get through.

This field became the Valley of Death for wounded men waiting for medicine.

When the Union began to fail at the Peach Orchard, Meade and Hancock, viewing the battle from Cemetery Ridge, sent all the reinforcements available—Hancock directed the fresh troops of II Corps to important positions in the areas of the Wheatfield and Peach Orchard, while Lieutenant Colonel Freeman McGilvery assembled batteries to the left and right to slow attacks. McGilvery met Barksdale's Brigade head-on, thwarting its progress toward the ridge—and Barksdale took a rifle shot to his left knee just before a cannonball hit his left foot, while a third bullet burrowed into his chest. Barksdale died the next morning in a Union field hospital.

Here at Plum Run, three Confederate brigades under Kershaw, Semmes, and Anderson saw victory in the Wheatfield and Peach Orchard and began to advance across Plum Run to attempt an attack on Little Round Top. The Union was ready for them, however, as a brigade of the V Corps led by Colonel William McCandless forced them back toward the Wheatfield, trapping them in this valley. Meanwhile, Brigadier General Frank Wheaton's brigade of the VI Corps discovered Wofford's Brigade advancing to the north, and hammered into them. In the ensuing fighting, bodies clad in blue and gray piled up here in the Valley of Death.

Today, a mowed path leads you around and through the peaceful valley, allowing you some time for quiet reflection as you cross the ground that once echoed with rifle shot, cannon fire, and the cries of the wounded and dying.

"I passed through the line waving my sword, shouting, 'Forward, men, to the ledge!' and promptly followed by the command in splendid style. We drove the Federals from their strong defensive position; five times they rallied and charged us, twice coming so near that some of my men had to use the bayonet, but in vain was their effort. It was our time now to deal death and destruction to a gallant foe, and the account was speedily settled."
—**Colonel William C. Oates, 15th Alabama Brigade**

Tour Stop 12: Pennsylvania Memorial

Union Victory at Cemetery Ridge

You've arrived on Cemetery Ridge, the long crest of high ground held by Union forces throughout the Battle at Gettysburg.

Here you can visit the Pennsylvania Monument, the largest in the park; its tablets bear names of all of the 34,500 men from Pennsylvania who fought at Gettysburg—roughly a third of the Union's entire military strength. Erected in 1910, the memorial features the Goddess of Victory and Peace standing 21 feet high at its top; the bronze used to create her came from actual cannonballs used in battle on this ground.

On July 2, with so many brigades and divisions sent to defend Little Round Top, the Wheatfield, and the Peach Orchard, the Union center at Cemetery Ridge became the weak spot in the Federal line. At about 7:00 p.m., General Hancock rode through here and spotted 1,700 Alabama soldiers heading for this area. Turning to see if the ridge had adequate defense, he discovered that there was only one Union regiment in proximity: the First Minnesota Volunteer Infantry, under Colonel William J. Colvill.

Hancock summoned his best skills of command and pointed to the Confederate flag on its way up the ridge. He shouted the order to Colvill, "Advance, Colonel, and take those colors!"

The 262–man Minnesota regiment fought the 1,700 Alabama soldiers in the woodlot to your left. More than 82 percent of the men from Minnesota

Minnesota soldiers held this ground on Cemetery Ridge at day's end, despite incredible odds.

Previous spread: The high
ground at Cemetery Ridge
now hosts the Pennsylvania
Monument.

died, were wounded, or missing in just a few minutes of battle, but their efforts met their mark—the
little Minnesota regiment stopped the Confederate
assault.

*"Every man realized in an instant what that order meant—
death or wounds to us all, the sacrifice of the regiment, to
gain a few minutes' time and save the position. And every
man saw and accepted the necessity for the sacrifice;
and in a moment, responding to Colvill's rapid orders,
the regiment, in perfect line, with arms, at 'right shoulder,
shift,' was sweeping down the slope directly upon the
enemy's centre. No hesitation, no stopping to fire, though
the men fell fast at every stride before the concentrated
fire of the whole Confederate force, directed upon us as
soon as the movement was observed."*
—**Lieutenant William Lochren, First Minnesota Infantry,
written January 1890**

Tour Stop 13: Spangler's Spring and Culp's Hill

The Long, Hard Fight to Win the Day

You're at the site of Spangler's Spring, a freshwater spring that provided a steady water supply to area residents for many decades before the Battle at Gettysburg. The Union's XII Corps under Brigadier General George S. Greene waited in reserve here throughout the morning and early afternoon of July 2, building a line of defense from here for half a

Spangler's Spring became a favorite stopping place for tourists.

"O, Mary, it is sad to look now at our shattered band of devoted men. Only four field officers in the brigade have escaped and I am one of them. I have no opportunity to say more now or write to any one else. Tell mother I am safe. God has been kind to me and I think he will spare me."

—Lt. Col. Rufus R. Dawes, 6th Wisconsin Infantry, to his wife, Mary, July 3, 1863

mile to the top of Culp's Hill—earthworks constructed of logs, rocks, and soil. (The earthworks you see here are accurate reproductions.)

In Lee's original plan for the fighting on July 2, Lieutenant General Ewell was to begin his attack on the Union's right flank at Culp's Hill as soon as he heard gunfire from Longstreet's advance on the Union left. But although Longstreet's attack began at about 4:00 p.m., Ewell and his men remained on Benner's Hill—about a mile northeast of Culp's Hill—and delivered an artillery barrage as a demonstration of force, meant to distract Meade from the far more destructive activity at the Union general's left flank.

Meade was not fooled, however, and he focused his energies and forces on the Peach Orchard and Wheatfield as the fighting there intensified. Meade sent troops from his interior line—the "barb" of the fishhook, which curled around Culp's Hill and back nearly to Cemetery Ridge—to support the defense of the Union high ground at the left flank. This left just about 1,300 Union soldiers of XII Corps here at Culp's Hill to face the unexpected attack by some 5,000 Confederates. As they were redeployed to the Wheatfield, the men of XII Corps had no choice but to leave their earthworks at Spangler's Spring undefended.

At about 7:00 p.m., Major General Edward "Allegheny" Johnson's division of Ewell's Second Corps advanced slowly on Culp's Hill, gaining some ground as they wore away at the single division of the Union's XII Corps, under Greene, that defended its position there. Greene sent for reinforcements from the XI and I Corps stationed

nearby, and they returned a total of 750 men—and, even more importantly, additional ammunition to replenish Greene's dwindling supplies.

Union breastworks held the day at Culp's Hill.

The confrontation for this hill involved some of the longest sustained fighting in the entire Battle of Gettysburg. The fighting finally ended as darkness fell, and the ensuing calm revealed that the Union force had surmounted incredible odds, maintaining control of the summit and inflicting many times more casualties than they received. The breastworks built by the men of XII Corps received considerable credit for the Union success on Culp's Hill.

When the remaining men of XII Corps finally returned after nightfall on July 2, they discovered that Brigadier General George "Maryland" Steuart's Brigade had occupied the breastworks and moved into their camp. An immediate skirmish broke out, but the Confederate brigade repelled it and held the position through the night. When the fighting came to a halt around 11:00 p.m., an unnatural quiet settled over the area—and Steuart's Brigade remained on high alert.

Now the Union held the high ground at Culp's Hill, however, and at about 4:00 a.m. on July 3, XII Corps attacked Steuart's Brigade from its stronger position. For the next three hours, the two corps fought for the hill and these breastworks.

As the fighting reached a climax near 7:00 a.m., two Union regiments—the Second Massachusetts and Twenty-seventh Indiana—were ordered in from the meadow nearby to support XII Corps in taking the breastworks back. Their attack was a catastrophe, as the 655 men from Massachusetts and Indiana were met by hidden Confederate marksmen, who gunned down 242 Union men in a matter of minutes.

Despite this momentary success, however, the Confederate forces could not gain ground after seven continuous hours of fighting for the breastworks and the hill. Finally, Major General Johnson ordered Steuart and his men to pull back. Steuart's Brigade had taken heavy casualties, with two regiments losing more than half of their men and his own Maryland Battalion down 189 soldiers. Steuart reluctantly relinquished the earthworks to the Union corps.

As you drive beyond Spangler's Spring and up Culp's Hill, you will come to an observation tower. Park here and climb the tower for a spectacular view of the area that formed the right end of the Union line.

Tour Stop 14: East Cemetery Hill

Tenacity Meets Its Match

You've arrived at Evergreen Cemetery, a privately owned community cemetery founded for Gettysburg residents in 1854. Among the many well-known citizens interred here are Virginia "Jennie" Wade, the only civilian killed during the Battle of Gettysburg; John Burns, the only Gettysburg civilian who volunteered to fight alongside the Union army during the battle; and William H. Tipton, one of the earliest battlefield photographers, whose

The cemetery gatehouse survived the Battle of Gettysburg.

work gives us some of the most vivid images of Gettysburg in the years after the battle.

While fighting raged on the right flank of the Union line at dusk on July 2, two Confederate brigades under General Jubal Early—the "Louisiana Tigers" of the Sixth, Seventh, and Ninth Regiments, and the Sixth North Carolina— charged to take East Cemetery Hill from the men of General Oliver Howard's XI Corps. You may recall that the Union's XI Corps regrouped here around noon of the first day of battle, after Confederate troops pushed them back through the town of Gettysburg to this point. Since then, Howard had made use of the stone walls that divided the hill into pastures, building additional earthworks as protective barriers against the attack to come.

Under cover of darkness and smoke from the battles to the west and south, Confederate brigades led by General Harry Hays, Colonel Isaac Avery, and Major Samuel Tate crossed half a mile of farmland, climbed over stone walls and pushed down split-rail fences to reach the well-fortified hill. The Union soldiers could not see the approaching 2,500 troops in the dark, but they could hear hundreds of feet on the march—so when the Confederates reached the base of the hill, rushed the stone walls and erupted with musket fire and rebel yells, the notorious XI Corps lost much of its nerve. Many Union soldiers panicked and ran, the Louisiana Confederates hot on their heels. In short order, the men of the Sixth North Carolina and Ninth Louisiana captured the Union's big guns.

Gettysburg

"Tell my father I died with my face to the enemy."
—Colonel Isaac Avery, in a note to Major Samuel Tate, shortly before Avery's death from a musket ball through the neck

Monuments to the Fifth Maine Infantry and Major General Henry Slocum dominate the view of Cemetery Hill.

General Hancock, watching from Cemetery Ridge, saw the chaos and ordered Colonel Samuel S. Carroll's brigade—part of II Corps—to rush to Cemetery Hill and restore Union control. The counterattack stemmed the Confederate tide, and by midnight on July 2, the men of II Corps drove the North Carolinians and Louisianans from the hill—but not before the Confederates lost more than 350 men in the battle.

Day 2 Ends with Monumental Losses

By the end of the day on July 2, nearly 18,000 more soldiers were dead, wounded or missing in action—roughly 9,000 on each side. The total losses for the two days of battle had already climbed to 33,500, 18,000 of whom were Union troops, while 15,500 fell from the Confederate ranks. Of the wounded, thousands lay in the Wheatfield, Peach Orchard, and the Valley of Death awaiting medical attention—many of whom would perish overnight.

General Meade met at his headquarters with the commanders of each corps that evening (except for Sickles, commander of III Corps, who remained in a field hospital after the amputation of his leg that afternoon), and determined that their strongest next move was to retain the Union position on the high ground. Overnight, the Union army reinforced its line from the Round Tops to Culp's Hill and Cemetery Hill, maintaining defensive strength while they waited to see what General Lee planned for July 3.

At the same time, Lee met with his officers in his headquarters on Seminary Ridge to assess their gains and losses and consider the next day's strategy. With so much fortification on either end of the Union line, Lee determined his best course of action: Longstreet and Ewell would return to each Union flank and continue to bombard these positions, while J.E.B. Stuart, the absent cavalry officer who arrived late on July 2, would march east and attempt to come at the Union flank from behind.

Lee and his officers met at the general's headquarters late on July 2.

The main attack of the day, however—one not in Lee's original plan—would strike the Union center, where Lee came to believe that Union forces were spread thinnest. This change in strategy in the morning hours became the turning point in the Civil War.

"Nothing today," said U.S. War Department officer Don Piatt's report to President Lincoln on July 2, 1863.

Day 3

Tour Stop 15: The High Water Mark

Pickett's Charge and the End of the Battle

At no other point in the Civil War did the Confederate army advance as far into Union territory as it did on July 3, when 12,000 men marched across the field beyond the stone wall to your left, in a display of courage and desperation known as Pickett's Charge. History calls this the "high water mark" of the Confederate advance, and it signifies both the Confederacy's northernmost penetration and the point at which it met its worst defeat to date, one that signaled the beginning of the end for the Army of Northern Virginia.

The Angle at Cemetery Ridge became the Confederates' undoing as they attempted to charge over it.

Battlefield photographer William Tipton captured the High Water Mark as it stood in 1910, a tribute to those who fought here.

Attempting to follow the orders Lee had set the night before, Ewell met with a surprise bombardment from Union troops that drove his corps off Culp's Hill by 11:00 a.m. Longstreet, meanwhile, misunderstood his orders and planned to *turn* the Federal left rather than attack it, so his troops were in the wrong position for a frontal assault.

Later in the morning, well east of the main battle, Major General J. E. B. Stuart—leading Lee's cavalry—realized that his planned advance on the Union rear had been spotted by Federal artillerymen, and quickly moved his men into columns to take on the enemy's counterattack. Brisk fighting broke out, both on foot in Rummel's Woods and on horseback, but Stuart's forces could not overcome the Union barrage—particularly that of a young officer in his first battle command, the hard-charging Brigadier General George Armstrong

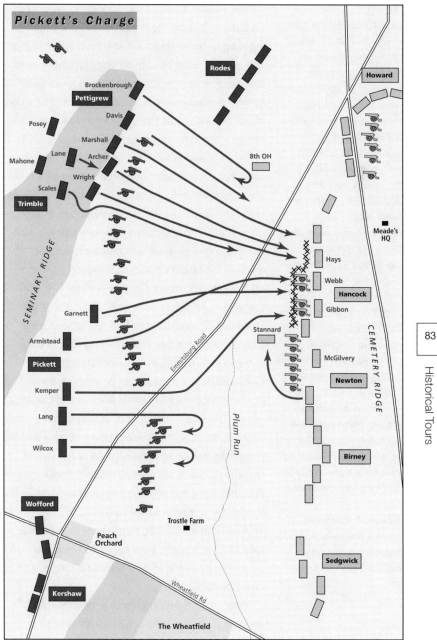

Pickett's Charge

Rodes

Howard

Brockenbrough

Pettigrew

Davis

Posey

Marshall

Mahone   Lane   Archer   8th OH

Wright

Scales

Trimble

SEMINARY RIDGE

Meade's HQ

Hays

Webb

Hancock

Gibbon

Garnett

Armistead   Stannard

McGilvery

Pickett

Kemper   Newton

CEMETERY RIDGE

Lang

Wilcox

Birney

Wofford

Trostle Farm

Peach Orchard

Plum Run

Emmitsburg Road

Kershaw

Wheatfield Rd

The Wheatfield

Sedgwick

Custer. Custer and his First Michigan Cavalry put up a much tougher fight than Stuart expected, giving no quarter when Stuart executed a last charge with sabers drawn and guns blazing. Custer and his men met him head-on, holding the Confederate cavalry at bay while the Third Pennsylvania Cavalry struck from the rear. Stuart had no choice but to retreat—another defeat for the Confederacy.

Lee, observing from Seminary Ridge and realizing that his original strategy had fallen by the wayside, quickly formulated a new plan: He would strike the Union center, the weakest part of the enemy line. The attack would begin with a heavy bombardment by Southern artillery to further weaken the Union's position, and then send men commanded by Major General George E. Pickett, General J. Johnston Pettigrew, and General Isaac Ridgeway Trimble directly forward, across a featureless open field, to break through the Union line.

At 1:00 p.m. on July 3, a concentration of 140 Confederate cannons began a two-hour barrage of gunfire on the middle of the Union line at Cemetery Ridge. The Union responded, aiming about eighty cannons back at the Confederate artillery—and the combined firepower generated so much smoke that the Confederate artillery officers could not tell that they were actually firing *beyond* and *above* the Union line, not hitting their targets.

At last, at about 3:00 p.m., more than 12,000 men in long, straight lines began to cross the open land—nearly a mile of land without a tree or rock to give the men cover.

Why Lee ordered such a charge remains a mystery. The year before, he had witnessed a spectacular Union defeat at Fredericksburg, when

A simple stone monument, flanked by Union artillery, marks the Confederate High Water Mark.

The Confederate army charged across this open field from Seminary Ridge, across the center of Gettysburg battlefield, in a last effort to overpower the Union.

Major General Ambrose Burnside of the Union army ordered exactly this kind of frontal, straight-line attack and it turned into a suicide march. Thousands of Union lives were lost while the Confederate army remained entrenched on its high ground, and Lee himself had watched in amazement and horror.

Nonetheless, led by Pickett, the entire Confederate force faced the Union solders across a great field of war, and were met by pounding cannon fire that began the destruction of their ranks. When the Confederates were in range, the Union line opened fire with rifles and muskets, watching in disbelief as Southern men fell by the hundreds . . . and another line emerged behind the first, continuing to advance until the first of them—led by Brigadier General Lewis Armistead—reached the Angle in the stone wall along Cemetery Ridge (to the left of the road) and attempted to scale the wall. Armistead was wounded almost immediately and died several days later; a small monument now stands on the spot where Armistead fell, in the middle of the Angle.

The Confederate force that managed to penetrate beyond the stone wall quickly fell to the musket fire and bayonets of Union men, whose position behind the wall protected them from major losses.

In just one hour, the frontal assault virtually halved the ranks of the advancing Confederates, with 6,555 dead, wounded, or missing by 4:00 p.m. Some Confederate regiments lost as many as 90 percent of their soldiers. Lee met the retreating men as they returned to Seminary Ridge, and was heard to insist, "This is my fault," over and over to the protesting men.

With so many soldiers and officers lost and his remaining men demoralized, Lee had little choice but to assume a defensive position, awaiting whatever final rout the Union army had in store. Meade, however, chose not to attack again. The Confederate army remained in its lines and sat out the day on July 4, but with no new Union offensive signaled, Lee made the decision to retreat back into Virginia, where he and his troops could regroup close to their supply lines. They withdrew in the rain that night, with no alternative but to abandon their dead and some of their wounded to the ministrations of merciful people in Gettysburg and the surrounding area.

With the three-day battle finally ended, both armies could begin to get a sense of their losses. Dead, wounded, and missing were 28,000 Confederate troops out of the 75,000 who arrived at Gettysburg, while the Union casualties were 23,000 out of their total 88,000 troops.

Under cover of rain and darkness, the Army of Northern Virginia withdrew on July 4.

The Aftermath

Tour Stop 16: Soldiers National Cemetery

"These dead shall not have died in vain."

What happened the day after the Battle of Gettysburg?

Confederate troops buried some of their dead, but with the urgent need to return to the comparative safety of their own territory, they had no choice but to leave their dead and some 7,500 wounded behind as they retreated toward Virginia. There was no time to provide adequate medical care, food, and water to the wounded who would travel with the retreating troops. Loaded onto wagons lacking even the most basic comfort of straw padding, these men rode in agony, their cries resounding along the entire retreating line as they appealed for water and relief from their pain.

Gettysburg had barely begun to realize that the battle had ended by the night of July 4. Agnes Barr, a Gettysburg resident, flew a white flag as she ran to nearby Cemetery Hill in the middle of the night to bring the first news of the Confederate retreat to Union troops there. The Federals moved quickly to round up the last Confederates in town and end the Southern occupation of Gettysburg.

Union soldiers began burying their dead, and many of the Confederate dead as well. Field hospitals were established in nearly every available building and home, with little concern over the color of any wounded man's uniform. The entire

city of Gettysburg joined to care for the wounded and bury the Confederate dead, while the Union army, already receiving orders to move to the next confrontation, stayed just long enough to bury their own comrades before marching from town.

"At Bull Run, I had seen only a very small scale what I was now to behold," wrote Major General Carl Schurz in his autobiography after the war. "At Gettysburg the wounded—many thousands of them—were carried to the farmsteads behind our lines. The houses, the barns, the sheds, and the open barnyards were crowded with moaning and wailing human beings, and still an unceasing procession of stretchers and ambulances was coming in from all sides to augment the number of the sufferers."

The result was that the countryside was filled with thousands of graves; it wasn't long before talk began of a new cemetery for those who had fallen at Gettysburg.

When the battle ended, bodies were scattered across fields and woods.

Facing page: The National Cemetery contains many graves of unknown soldiers who fell at Gettysburg.

Historical Tours

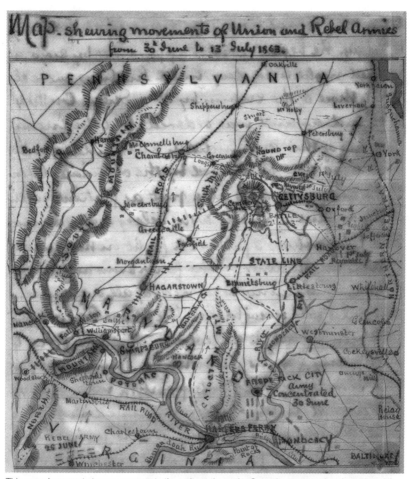

This map documents troop movements throughout the entire Gettysburg campaign, from June 30 through July 13—including the weeks following the battle. Casualties continued to mount after July 3 as the Union army pursued the Confederates, bringing the total number of dead, wounded, and missing to 51,000.

While the bodies of Union soldiers had been buried, most graves were crudely marked at best, making it desperately difficult for families who came to claim the bodies of their loved ones to even locate the final resting places of their brothers, husbands, and sons. Other graves would be lost in a short time because their hastily scribbled cardboard headstones could not last the winter.

Determining that a soldiers' cemetery was required, Gettysburg residents Theodore Dimon, a doctor, and David Wills, an attorney who represented Pennsylvania, took the first steps to make such hallowed ground a reality. Wills proposed this to Pennsylvania governor Andrew Curtin, and they navigated local land politics to develop the Soldiers National Cemetery for the Union troops who had fallen at Gettysburg. Later, in the 1870s, the bodies of fallen Confederate soldiers were exhumed from the fields on which they had died, and transported to cemeteries in the South for final interment.

More than 10,000 people attended the dedication of Soldiers National Cemetery on November 19, 1863. Edward Everett, a well-known orator of the time, delivered the central speech of the dedication: a two-hour-long treatise that made a sweeping journey through every significant event of the war to date, nearly paralyzing those who stood and listened to his entire lecture. As an afterthought, Wills invited President Abraham Lincoln to speak.

Lincoln's three-minute, 256-word speech followed the Everett oration. Firsthand accounts note that the president was interrupted five times for applause, although when he left the rock on which he stood to deliver the address, the audience response was one of stunned silence, with just a

"But . . . we can not dedicate—we can not consecrate—we can not hallow, this ground—The brave men, living and dead, who struggled here, have hallowed it, far above our poor power to add or detract. The world will little note, nor long remember what we say here, while it can never forget what they did here."

—President Abraham Lincoln, November 19, 1863

smattering of applause. Lincoln interpreted this to mean that his words had failed. History chooses to differ with his impression, however: The Gettysburg Address rose to become the most famous speech ever given to date by an American president, one that students now analyze and memorize in classrooms across the country more than 150 years after its first and only delivery. Today, a monument stands on the place where Lincoln delivered this address.

As for the renamed Gettysburg National Cemetery, the grounds now include burial places of American veterans from all of the major wars and conflicts faced by the United States since the Civil War.

A monument stands on the spot where Lincoln gave the Gettysburg Address.

Alfred Waud: The Civil War's Great Illustrator

When Alfred Rudolph Waud arrived in the United States from his native England in 1850, he did not intend to become the foremost artist and illustrator of the American Civil War—he had his sights set on theatrical scene painting. His aspirations changed significantly when he took a full-time position as "special artist" for the *New York Illustrated News:* Following the Army of the Potomac from the first Battle of Bull Run (Manassas) in 1861 to the Battle of Petersburg in 1865, he captured the Civil War in drawings on brown paper. Today, these illustrations provide some of history's most vivid depictions of the war as it happened.

Gettysburg: A Tourist's Guide to Exploring, Staying, and Eating

ENRICHING YOUR EXPERIENCE BEYOND THE BATTLEFIELD

While Gettysburg National Military Park preserves the battlefield itself, the town of Gettysburg provides a rich historical context that highlights the days of battle, the local residents who played key roles before, during, and after the fighting, and the battle's place in the Civil War timeline. Extend your knowledge and experience of the epic battle and its effect on this small town—with a population of just 2,500 in 1863—and see the war through the eyes of civilians whose lives were changed forever by the fighting waged on this ground.

Battlefield Tours with Licensed Battlefield Guides, Museum and Visitor Center at Gettysburg National Military Park, 97 Taneytown Road, (877) 874-2478, (717) 338-1243, www.gettysburgtour guides.org. Nov–Mar, daily 8–6; Apr–Oct, daily 8–7. Two-hour tour $55 for 1–6 people; see Web site for other rates. Tour the battlefield while a Licensed Battlefield Guide rides with you in your vehicle and tells you the story of the Battle of Gettysburg in as much detail as you would like.

Downtown Historic Walking Tour, Destination Gettysburg: (800) 337-5015, www.gettysburg. travel. Self-guided. Free. Pick up a tour brochure at one of Destination Gettysburg's visitor centers (35 Carlisle Street or at the Gettysburg National Military Park Visitor Center) and visit thirty-two historic sites

Lincoln statue in front of the David Wills House

throughout the town at your own pace. You'll walk the path President Lincoln took on his way to the dedication of the National Cemetery, and you'll discover the people and places that played supporting roles in the battle and its aftermath.

Eisenhower National Historic Site, 97 Taneytown Road, (717) 338-9114, www.nps.gov/eise. Daily 9–4; closed Thanksgiving, Christmas, and New Year's Day. Adults $7.50, ages 6–12 $5. Adjacent to the Gettysburg battlefield, the home and farm of President Dwight D. Eisenhower served as a weekend retreat for the president and his family, as well as a place to meet with and entertain leaders from all over the world. Tour the modest farmhouse and enjoy a walk around the working farmyard, where cattle still graze and Eisenhower's own vehicles stand in the garage. To reach the farm, you must take a bus from the Gettysburg National Military Park Visitor Center.

Take a bus from the Gettysburg visitor center to visit the home of Dwight Eisenhower.

This stone house gave General Lee and his officers a meeting place on July 2, 1863.

General Lee's Headquarters Museum, 401 Buford Avenue, (717) 334-3141, www.civilwar headquarters.com. Mar–Nov, daily 9–5. Adults $3, youth 15 and under $1. General Robert E. Lee conferred with his officers in this building on the morning and evening of July 2, 1863. Today this museum hosts living history encampments on summer weekends and houses an impressive collection of Civil War artifacts.

Gettysburg Battle Theatre, 425 Steinwehr Avenue, (717) 334-6100, www.gettysburgaddress .com/HTMLS/Museum.html. Mar–Nov, daily 9–5; extended hours in summer; closed Dec–Feb. This animated multimedia presentation provides a credible overview of battle line formation and maneuvers during the three days at Gettysburg.

Gettysburg Battlefield Tours, 778 Baltimore Street, (717) 334-6296, www.gettysburgbattle fieldtours.com. Nov–Mar, daily 8–6; Apr–Oct, daily 8–7. Adults $26, ages 6–12 $15. Take a two-hour tour on a comfortable, air-conditioned or open-air bus with narration provided by a Licensed Battle-field Guide. Or choose the Dramatized Audio Tour, with a recorded narration complete with the roar of cannons and bugles sounding the call to battle.

Take the double-decker bus for a more comfortable two-hour tour of the battlefield.

Gettysburg Heritage Center, 297 Steinwehr Avenue, (717) 334-6245, www.gettysburgmuseum .com. Mar–Dec, daily 9–5; Jan–Feb, weekend and holidays 9–5; extended hours in summer. Adults $5.50, ages 6–17 $3. Formerly the American Civil War Wax Museum, this newly renovated center focuses on the town of Gettysburg and its heri-tage before, during, and after the battle. Historical documents, artifacts, and interactive displays tell the stories of ordinary townspeople thrust into situ-ations that challenged them in ways they could not have imagined. One of the area's best gift shops is here as well.

Ghosts of Gettysburg Tours, 271 Baltimore Street, (717) 337-0445, www.ghostsofgettysburg .com. Apr–Oct daily at dusk, Mar and Nov Friday and Saturdays only at dusk; call for exact tour times. $9.50–$10, ages 2 and under free. You'll find many ghost-tour operators from which to choose in town, now that cable television shows have declared Gettysburg a hot spot for para-

99

Exploring, Staying, and Eating

Nearly every building in the town of Gettysburg has its own story to share.

normal activity. Ghosts of Gettysburg bases its tours on the best-selling books by Mark Nesbitt, a former National Park Service ranger who founded this organization. Whatever you may believe, you'll have a terrifically creepy time on a candlelight walking tour with a well-versed guide.

Hall of Presidents, 789 Baltimore Street, (717) 334-5717, www.gettysburgbattlefieldtours.com/ gettysburg-tours/museum-hall-of-presidents-first-ladies/the-hall-of-presidents. Mar–Nov, daily 9–5; extended hours in summer; closed Dec–Feb. Adults $7.50, children 6–12 $3.50, free to children 5 and under. Touted as the only museum to feature a complete wax collection of American presidents and their first ladies, this museum features life-size figures of the presidents and one-third-sized figures of the first ladies in their inaugural gowns. Background murals depicting the development of the United States are the work of contemporary artist Charles Morganthaler.

Jennie Wade House, 242–246 Baltimore Street, (717) 334-6020, www.gettysburgbattlefieldtours .com/Wade.html. Mar–Nov, weekdays 9–5, Fri and Sat 9–6.; extended hours in summer; closed Dec–Feb. Adults $8, ages 6–12 $4. Jennie Wade was baking bread in the kitchen of her sister's house on July 3, 1863, when a bullet found her and made her the only civilian killed during the battle. The house has been preserved as it appeared on that day.

Lincoln Train Museum, 425 Steinwehr Avenue, (717) 334-5678, www.lincolntrain.com. Apr-Sep, daily 9–9, Labor Day–Nov, Su–Th 9–6, F-Sa 9–8;

Dec–Mar, Th–M 10–6, closed Tu–W. Adults $7, ages 65+ $5, ages 6–12 $4, free ages 5 and under. Celebrate the spirit of Lincoln and the spirit of America at the renovated train museum, as a live re-enactor brings President Lincoln to life to tell tales of American history. The museum's legendary toy train collection features model trains that date back to the earliest days of the U.S. railroad.

Segway Tours of Gettysburg, 22 Springs Ave., (717) 253-7987, (888) 473-4868, www.segtours .com. Tour departure times: Mar 9:30 and 1:30, Apr–Aug 8:30, 12:30 and 4:30; Sep–Oct 7:30, 11:30 and 3:30, Nov 8:30 and 12:30. $70 western battlefield, $50 eastern battlefield. Take an in-depth look at Gettysburg battlefield from an unusual perch on a Segway. The guided tour makes a leisurely exploration of areas including the Wheatfield, Devil's Den, and Little Round Top. The novelty alone makes this a great choice on a pretty spring or fall day.

Soldier's National Museum, 777 Baltimore Street, (717) 334-4890, www.gettysburgbattlefieldtours .com/Soldiers.html. Mar–Nov, daily 9–5; extended hours in summer; closed Dec–Feb. Adults $7.50, ages 6–12 $3.50. Explore the life-size Confederate encampment diorama and the collection of Civil War artifacts in the building used by Union Major General Oliver Otis Howard as his headquarters during the three-day battle.

Many buildings in downtown Gettysburg have been here since before the war—and you can enjoy them as shops, inns, and restaurants. (See p. 106 for restaurant details.)

Exploring, Staying, and Eating

WHERE TO STAY IN GETTYSBURG

You'll find some of your favorite hotel chains fairly close to town and to the battlefield—the Quality Inn at General Lee's Headquarters is just across from the park's tour road, while a brand-new Wyndham Gettysburg and a Courtyard by Marriott are about 8 miles from town. For a true sense of the town's genteel history, however, you may want to try one of these fine establishments, each of which offers a civilian's perspective of what it was like to live in Gettysburg before, during, and after the battle.

Brafferton Inn Bed & Breakfast, 44 York Street, (717) 337-3423, www.brafferton.com. Seventeen unique rooms, decorated individually with quiet, comforting colors accented with bold floral or

The Brafferton Inn offers quiet comfort with a historic flavor.

paisley comforters and shams, painted woods, and plenty of pillows, make this in-town inn a favorite with its many repeat guests. A full, home-cooked breakfast is included in your room rate, and some rooms feature Jacuzzi tubs.

The Fairfield Inn, West Main Street, Fairfield, (717) 642-5410, www.thefairfieldinn.com. Eight miles west of Gettysburg, this Fairfield is not part of the Marriott chain of the same name—in fact, it was built in 1757 and remains one of the nation's oldest continuously operated inns. Sleep where Major General J. E. B. Stuart rested his head during the retreat, or try a meal created from the recipes used when the innkeeper fed General Robert E. Lee and his officers on July 4, 1863. This National Register of Historic Places member deserves a stop—and once you've seen it, you'll want to stay for a meal or a night.

The Gaslight Inn, 33 East Middle Street, (717) 337-9100, www.thegaslightinn.com. This 1872 bed-and-breakfast offers nine well-appointed, airy rooms with private baths; some have fireplaces. Jacuzzi tubs and steam sauna showers give this three-story house a sense of luxury, while the outdoor pond and breezy front porch hearken back to its nineteenth-century roots.

Gettysburg Hotel, 1 Lincoln Square, (717) 337-2000, (866) 378-1797, www.hotelgettysburg.com. Established in 1797 and still the most recognizable hotel in town, the Gettysburg Hotel maintains its well-established reputation for quality by skillfully combining old and new. The Centuries on the Square restaurant feels like a colonial tavern's

The Gettysburg Hotel is the most famous in town.

dining room, and McClellan's Tavern's rosy walls and walnut wainscoting preserve the sense of a simpler time. Upstairs, you'll find modern rooms with Internet access and full cable TV service in every guest room. Luxury suites offer fireplaces and Jacuzzi tubs, and efficiency suites provide kitchens to help accommodate families.

The Inn at Herr Ridge, 900 Chambersburg Road (Pennsylvania Highway 30 West), (800) 362-9849, (717) 334-4332, www.innatherrridge.com. Listed on the National Register of Historic Places, this establishment first opened in 1815 as a tavern, and it offered lodging for the first time in 1828. During the Civil War, it served as a hospital as the battle raged around it. Today this inn features seventeen distinctive rooms and suites, as well as a tavern for casual dining and a fine restaurant.

James Gettys Hotel, 27 Chambersburg Street, (717) 337-1334, (888) 900-5275, www.james gettyshotel.com. You may have guessed that Gettys founded Gettysburg, and this downtown suite-style hotel has been restored to its 1920s appearance with tastefully floral wallpaper and polished wood trim, wood or iron bedsteads in comfortably large rooms, and modern kitchenettes with refrigerators and microwaves as well as cooking areas. Note that this is a nonsmoking hotel.

The Gettys Hotel combines 1860s architecture with 1920s style.

WHERE TO EAT IN GETTYSBURG

Blue & Gray Bar & Grill, 2 Baltimore St., (717) 334-1999, www.bluegraybargrill.com. All of your bar food favorites are here, including twenty-five variations on the chicken wing and twelve specialty burgers. The menu of appetizers alone provides plenty of variety, from mussels steamed in white wine and garlic to fresh jalapeno peppers stuffed with cheese and wrapped in bacon. You won't leave hungry.

Dobbin House Tavern, 89 Steinwehr Avenue, in the springhouse, behind the bed-and-breakfast of the same name, (717) 334-2100, www.dobbin house.com. Step carefully down the stone stairs into this dim, nearly underground tavern, where candles seem to provide the only light and hushed conversations rustle toward you through the

Candlelight illuminates the Dobbin House Tavern, one of the oldest in town.

gloom. You'll swear that time stopped in 1776 as a barmaid in period dress leads you to a booth with high, polished oak sides, and offers you a menu on stiff brown paper. Have no fear: Despite the quaint spelling of "sallade," the dishes are fresh and modern with a colonial touch—try Dobbin's hot beef sandwich, served au jus, or the crispy, juicy spit-roasted chicken. Save room for warm gingerbread with lemon sauce, or a slice of "pye."

Historic Farnsworth House Inn, 401 Baltimore Street, (717) 334-8838, www.farnsworthhouseinn .com. Pennsylvania Dutch flavors mix with past and current Gettysburg history in this remarkable tavern, where you can sit outside on the ivy-covered patio or inside in the warm, inviting dining room. Try the slippery chicken potpie, a comfort food favorite involving thick noodles in a chunky chicken sauce. A fat slab of Aunt Ann's meatloaf arrives with dark gravy and hand-mashed potatoes, and even your hot dog gets a local twist, covered in chili, onions, and mustard. When you top off your meal with a slice of shoofly pie or walnut apple cake, you won't leave hungry.

Mr. G's Ice Cream, 404 Baltimore St., (717) 334-7600, facebook.com/pages/Mr-Gs. You'll find this parlour in the historic Twin Sycamores house, where you can see bullet holes from the battle and enjoy delicious homemade ice cream. Fans advise that you try the salted caramel flavor, but you'll have plenty of choices no matter what you want to sample. Take a pleasant walk after dinner in town to find this charming confectioner.

Enjoy the enormous selection of good food at the Pub & Restaurant.

The Pub & Restaurant, 20 Lincoln Square #22, (717) 334-7100, www.the-pub.com. You can't miss this restaurant right on Lincoln Square, and you won't want to—the humongous menu ranges from inventive salads like Bob's Pinwheel, a feast of deli meats and vegetables topped with pinwheel pasta, to "jacket wraps" and Brent's Pub Club, a mountain of ham, capicola, salami, bacon, Swiss, provolone, and lettuce and tomato, piled on alternating layers of rye and pumpernickel. Seafood and steak entrees and as southern a pecan pie as you will find north of New Orleans make this one of the most entertaining places in town for lunch or dinner.

Glossary

artillery: The military organization in charge of the largest weapons, including cannons. Artillery officers and their men—often called gunners—are experts in the correct and accurate discharge of these weapons, as well as the transportation of big guns to the battle site.

battalion: A military unit containing two or more companies from a parent regiment. For example, a regiment would contain ten companies (A through K), and a battalion from that regiment might contain A, C and F company.

brigade: A military unit that is smaller than a division but equal to a regiment. Civil War brigades were commanded by a colonel, and often contained 3,000 or more soldiers.

cavalry: A unit of soldiers who fight on horseback.

corps: A large formation of troops with a common function, commanded by major generals. The U.S. Army of the Potomac had six corps organizations, each with 10,000 to 15,000 soldiers. The Confederate army's corps were larger than those of the Union army, sometimes containing 20,000 soldiers.

division: A large military unit, usually containing several regiments or brigades. Several divisions make up a corps. Training, administration, and tactical functions all took place at the division level.

fishhook: An ingenious battle formation chosen by Major General George Meade that allowed him to reinforce his main line of defense from a protected interior line, one layer removed from the fighting. This strategy is one of the main elements credited with Meade's success at Gettysburg.

flank: The extreme end of the Union's or Confederates' battle line. The Union's left and right flanks were critical offensive targets for the Confederacy, as they were perceived as the weakest points in the Union's defensive line.

infantry: Soldiers trained to fight on foot, rather than on horseback.

regiment: A military unit commanded by a colonel, containing three battalions and a headquarters company. A regiment can range in size from a few hundred to several thousand soldiers.

salient: A military position in which the defending army creates a line of attack that projects into enemy territory, leaving the line vulnerable on three sides. This is usually an unintentional formation (as was the case with Major General Daniel Sickles's salient at the Peach Orchard).

script: Money issued by the Confederate States of America. Outside of the states that had seceded from the Union, script had no value.

secede: The withdrawal from a political organization, such as a country. The Confederate states seceded from the United States over issues of states' rights.

Bibliography

Black, Linda Giberson. *Gettysburg Remembers President Lincoln: Eyewitness Accounts of November 1863.* Gettysburg, Pa.: Thomas Publications, 2005.

Chamberlain, Joshua Lawrence. *Bayonet! Forward! My Civil War Reminiscences.* Gettysburg, Pa.: Stan Clark Military Books, 1994.

Coco, Gregory A. *On the Bloodstained Field.* Gettysburg, Pa.: Thomas Publications, 1987.

———. *On the Bloodstained Field II.* Gettysburg, Pa.: Thomas Publications, 1989.

Evans, Clement Anselm. *Confederate Military History: A Library of Confederate States History.* Atlanta, Ga.: Confederate Pub. Co., 1899.

Flagel, Thomas R., and Ken Allers Jr. *The History Buff's Guide to Gettysburg.* Nashville, Tenn.: Cumberland House Publishing, Inc., 2006.

Lochren, Lieutenant William. "The First Minnesota at Gettysburg" in *Glimpses of the Nation's Struggle.* Minnesota Military Order of the Loyal Legion of the United States (MOLLUS) vol. 3. New York: D. D. Merrill Company, 1893.

Longstreet, Helen D. *Lee and Longstreet at High Tide: Gettysburg In the Light of the Official Records.* Gainesville, Ga.: published by the author, 1904.

Mingus, Scott L., Sr. *Human Interest Stories of the Gettysburg Campaign.* Orrtanna, Pa.: Colecraft Industries, 2006.

———. *Human Interest Stories of the Gettysburg Campaign, Volume II.* Orrtanna, Pa.: Colecraft Industries, 2007.

Norton, Oliver Wilcox. *The Attack and Defense of Little Round Top, Gettysburg, July 2, 1863.* New York: The Neale Publishing Company, 1913.

Sessarego, Alan, from the collection of. *Letters Home V: Gettysburg!* Gettysburg, Pa.: Americana Souvenirs & Gifts, 2003.

Sheldon, George. *When the Smoke Cleared at Gettysburg: The Tragic Aftermath of the Bloodiest Battle of the Civil War.* Nashville, Tenn.: Cumberland House Publishing, Inc., 2003.

Stackpole, Edward J., and Wilbur S. Nye, revised by Bradley M. Gottfried. *The Battle of Gettysburg: A Guided Tour.* Gettysburg, Pa.: Americana Souvenirs & Gifts in association with Stackpole Books, 1998.

Stackpole, Edward J. *They Met at Gettysburg.* Gettysburg, Pa.: Stackpole Books, 1982.

Symonds, Craig L. *Gettysburg: A Battlefield Atlas.* Baltimore, Md.: The Nautical & Aviation Pub. Co., 1992.

Wills, Gary. *Lincoln at Gettysburg: The Words That Remade America.* New York: Simon and Schuster, 1992.

Index